CHILDREN, CELEBRATE

Children, Celebrate!

Resources For Youth Liturgy

by
Sister Maria Rabalais, C.S.J.
Rev. Howard Hall

PAULIST PRESS
NEW YORK ● PARAMUS ● TORONTO

Copyright © 1974 by
The Missionary Society
of St. Paul the Apostle
in the State of New York

All rights reserved. No part of this book may be reproduced or transmitted in any form or by any means, electronic or mechanical, including photocopying, recording or by any information storage and retrieval system, without permission in writing from the Publisher.

Design: Ellen Kenny
Library of Congress
Catalog Card Number: 73-94212

ISBN: 0-8091-1820-3

Published by Paulist Press
Editorial Office: 1865 Broadway, N.Y., N.Y. 10023
Business Office: 400 Sette Drive, Paramus, N.J. 07652

Printed and bound in the
United States of America

CONTENTS

Introduction 1

The Why and How of Children's Worship 3

Implementing a Program of Children's Worship 9

General Guidelines 15

    Themes 16
    Readings 17
    Prayers 20
    Setting 23
    Music 27
    Audio-Visuals 31
    Activity 36
    Specific Suggestions 40

Planning Sheet for a Eucharist 45

Sample Liturgies 49

    Primary Grades 49

        Creation: Our Beautiful World 50
        Good Example: Follow the Leader 54
        Festivals: Thanksgiving 58
        Church Year: Christmas 63
        Sacraments: First Communion 66

    Intermediate Grades 71

        Creation: Light 72
        Relationships: Friendship 76
        Festivals: Scout Sunday 79
        Church Year: All Saints 83
        Sacraments: First Penance 86

Junior High School 89

Creation: Life   90
Relationships: Loneliness   94
Festivals: End of the School Year   97
Church Year: Advent   100
Sacraments: Confirmation   103

Senior High School   107

Creation: Ecology   108
Relationships: Communication   112
Festivals: Fourth of July   115
Church Year: Easter   118
Sacraments: Marriage   121

Appendix   125

Suggested Themes for Liturgies   125
Music Bibliography   131
Bibliography   135

INTRODUCTION

The unique nature of a child's prayer life and his concepts of God is certainly familiar to the parent who has tried family prayer, to the priest who has heard children's confessions, and to the catechist who shares good news. Catechesis for children builds up their budding faith life slowly. The response of such faith, expressed in personal prayer and community liturgy, is best developed at a similar pace, according to the level of the child.

We rejoice that children's worship material is being spread by means of a multitude of sources. Frequent articles in *The Catechist* and *Religion Teachers Journal* enrich our work. Publishers of catechetical materials provide rich sources, for example, the latest book of *Celebrations* by Christiane Brusselmans and Brian Haggerty (Silver Burdett, 1972) and the *Let Us Pray* series by Robert Heyer, Jean Marie Hiesberger and Bernadette Kenny (Paulist Press, 1973). Publishers of liturgical material are beginning to respond to the needs of children, as is evidenced by publications from the Liturgical Conference, North American Liturgy Resources, and Paulist Press. The youth music field has been swarming—particularly on the adolescent level—with all manner of songs for worship. Names like Clarence Rivers, Sister Germaine, Joe Wise, and the Dameans have become household words. There is an equally long and impressive list of liturgical services, music, catechetical and sermon materials from dozens of Protestant publishers geared to youth worship.

It is our hope through *Children, Celebrate!* to synthesize some of the principles, approaches and sample models available for children's worship. We feel that the rationale behind such worship will help to give confidence to those afraid of venturing into the field of experimental liturgy. The approaches can strengthen people who feel that they cannot adequately relate a worship experience to the psyche and experience of young children and youth. The sample models presented here offer concrete examples of the possibilities of worship for youth and children. They can be used as given—or better, expanded upon and adapted—to render fitting praise flowing from the life experience of young people.

We likewise hope to encourage and clarify the efforts of many individuals working all over the land, and to prepare the way for the universal and official acceptance of a separate children's worship as a valid and rich expression of their beginning faith.

We believe that the significance of a child's grace life is initially expressed as he enters the Christian community through baptism. This life is nourished through the Eucharist which always remains central no matter what else has changed in the Church.

The Sacred Congregation of Divine Worship reinforces this concept with its new Directory for Masses with Children, issued November 1, 1973. Such a reaffirmation is encouraging and hopeful for the adults and students who have invested much time and effort in the liturgical movement. The liturgies that follow represent experiences that were spiritually enriching and professionally rewarding for those who planned and celebrated them.

This book requires a special note of appreciation to our committee colleagues for their significant contribution: Rev. Kenneth Baker, Sister Bonaventure, M.H.S., Ms. Bobbye Le Blanc, Dr. Wilbur Clarke, Rev. Michael Moroney, Ms. Eunice Royal, Rev. Sidney Becnel. Their creative effort in adapting these liturgies in prayerful experiences in their school and parish communities have been immensely valuable. In particular, we also want to acknowledge Ms. Mercedes Broussard, who read the final draft of the manuscript with care and made helpful suggestions. We are grateful to all persons without whose help this book would not have been possible. Finally, we are indebted to Robert Heyer for his genuine interest in our goal—"to celebrate children's growing faith in meaningful liturgies."

>Sister Maria Rabalais, C.S.J.
>Rev. Howard Hall
>Baton Rouge, Louisiana

THE WHY AND HOW OF CHILDREN'S WORSHIP

THE "WHY" OF CHILDREN'S WORSHIP

"To deviate from routine; to hold up for public acclaim, to enter into religious festivity" is to celebrate. And that has always been an intimate and vital part of man's life.

There was the paint and costume of primitive man as he prepared for the hunt and his dance at its culmination. Magnificent art, architecture and coffin treasures surrounded the burial of the pharoah. The thank offering of Pilgrim and Indian marked the early American scene. The contemporary head shop with candles, oils and incense for meditation serves the same need. Almost every ebb and beat of man's heart is ritualized.

Man's most common, or perhaps his most heightened experiences, center around the key passages of life: cigars at birth, the perennial birthday cake, the elaborate marriage preparations, the gold retirement watch, the mixed fellowship, food, and the flowers of the death ritual.

The fast pace of daily life in our burgeoning culture has added plasticity and impersonalness to blurr the humanness—and the sacredness—of these moments. The proud mother and father are separated from their newborn in the name of hygiene. We can afford to forget the birthday and pick up a "belated" card at the shopping center. The retirement is listed in "telephone book print" in the corporation newspaper and the mausoleum with its plastic flowers (permanent, they call them) glosses over the beauty of nature's life—death—life cycle.

To the credit of sensitive man today and the glory of Christian man, many still find time to pause to reflect on the meaning and quality of life. In savoring these moments, man sees their complex and intricate beauty and becomes increasingly aware of the miracles involved. He is caught up in the majesty and moved by what he experiences. He wants to dance, to sing, to be quiet, to write, to share. So he celebrates the occasion in liturgy.

Recent theological writings furnish us with new insights into the meaning and dignity of human life, as they indicate the impact of Christ becoming man, taking flesh and fusing the divine and the human. Scripture scholars help us to probe the beauty and the humanness of man struggling toward dialogue with his God. We deepen our awareness of God speaking to man through the events of history. Religious educators want us to realize that God is still announcing his good news by man's contemporary participation in the revelatory process. The glory of God and the goodness of creation expressed in Genesis 1 or Psalm 148 can also be "prayed" through the song of a mother at the kitchen sink or through dance steps before the altar.

Adult man celebrates his daily life in many distinct rituals: coffee breaks, fishing trips, bridge games, camping trips. Very often his "God experience" grows in these simple life rituals. In sharing a doughnut the broken eucharistic bread flashes to mind. As the bridge game gossip progresses, a scripture text is called to mind. The quiet after the campfire allows a hymn to greet the twinkling stars.

Liturgy builds up such experiences. It affords man the opportunity to ritualize and celebrate in community the totality of his existence in faith—at once divine and human.

The experience of adult faith is celebrated within the context of a structure, a set of symbols, and a terminology that is intelligible to a grown person. The adult is part of a faith community that has come to believe in a mature manner, to respond to faith in Christian commitment, and to express its belief in worship.

Children, on the other hand, have a distinct way of celebrating life on many formal and informal occasions. On an informal level, children celebrate life in their daily play activities. Birthdays, dances, holidays, and similar occasions are provided for by adults, but usually adapted to the life style of the young group celebrating.

If it is true, as most religious educators and common experience indicate, that faith is an adult virtue—one requiring powers of abstraction, experiences of life and love, possibilities of denial and betrayal beyond the experience of a child—then we must speak of faith for a child in terms of "beginning faith." In this context it is important for the child to glean the basis of faith from such informal experiences as acceptance, patience, change, and growth. These are most likely to occur informally on the playground and in the home—parental love, the death of a pet, a birthday party. It is also important to provide more formal, shared community experiences within the catechetical context.

Moreover, it is exceedingly important that the liturgical prayer experience of the child be celebrated within the context of a structure, a set of symbols, and a terminology that is more properly theirs, namely, a children's liturgy. The young child is just beginning to approach belief and is still very much a part of his immediate environment with its own attitudes, symbols, tastes, and values. So too, the awe and prayerfulness of the moment are most effectively expressed in a worship natural to his life style.

Two elements can be isolated in the process of children's growth in faith: community and prayer.

Community: In the average day a variety of community experiences are provided the child, the two prime ones being family and peers. The family provides a rich variety of possible relationships and growth experiences from a visit from grandma to the newly arrived baby. The relative sameness of the peer group provides a different type of growth experience and a whole new set of relationships, whether in the freer community of the playground or the more structured classroom experience.

Good community relationships among family or peers will take into consideration the uniqueness of each person, never forcing regimentation but inspiring creativity. It will foster in each child the opportunity to share in story, product, dance, and presence the talent that he possesses.

Each of these communities can actualize human and Christian growth and lead to an understanding of what it means to be brothers and sisters of the Lord and living members of the one body, his Church.

Prayer: Good communication and response come to be understood by children as they grow in experience through their families, classmates, and other communities. They also experience the consequences of non-communication which results from not listening or misunderstanding. Effective faith growth through catechesis and liturgy will work through, and not try to cover up, the tensions that arise. Thus, it will foster the experience of forgiveness, restoration of communication, and the accessibility of God to man. Such experiences are helpful in probing the meaning of prayer, seen as talking and listening to God, in much the same manner that they communicate and celebrate with family and friends.

Despite the fact that the dynamics of children's faith bring out the clear need for intelligible children's worship, we find that children are fed a steady diet of prayers and rituals with words and symbols quite unintelligible and meaningless to them. Canned and adult worship forms insure conformity at the expense of the principles of meaningful children's worship: simplicity of form, spontaneity in execution and community in expression. The continued use of irrelevant forms of worship for children and high school youth can only lead to confusion, boredom, and ultimate frustration rather than to a vital faith life and prayer experience.

It has been our experience that poor liturgies for our youth happen not because of lack of understanding of these principles and the needs of children, nor because of the lack of goodwill by parents, priests or teachers, but because of the need for practical "know how" in the preparation and execution of children's worship.

THE "HOW" OF CHILDREN'S WORSHIP

The team: We have noted that the beginnings of faith for the child grow and are cultivated within a community experience. A model of what the child can become already exists within the class, home or parish family. Here, the catechist, parents, and priests are the key leaders.

With this in mind, it is most important that these adult leaders work closely together as a "team" to provide a common understanding and experience for the child. They must share common goals and create meaningful prayer and liturgical experiences at home, school, and church. Such team effort requires, as its basis, an understanding of the *principles* of children's worship, namely, *simplicity* of form, *spontaneity* in execution and *community* in expression.

Principle one: simplicity of form. Children must be able to grasp the unity and meaning of the overall action with emphasis on the basic elements: WORD and EUCHARIST.

God continually reveals himself to man and he does it in a special way at this WORD SERVICE. Members of the worshipping community should be able to receive that revelation. Consequently, in preparing for the event, words should be chosen which are *intelligible* (paraphrasing and drama are helpful); words that *nourish* (scriptural concepts should be the basis, although other literary works could be introduced); words that *challenge* growth (this can be effectively done through the homily).

Secondly, the EUCHARISTIC MEAL or SACRIFICE is an exchange of gifts. Food offerings representing ourselves are offered to our Father through Christ, our brother, in his sacrifice. Jesus is contained, offered, received. Just as food is real to us, providing an opportunity to share and to grow, so too the Eucharist must free us to share and grow. Keep the community of children in mind by making the gifts real. Can they see what you're offering? Pass it around. Let them present something. The consecratory prayer should be intelligible and brief. "Linus, Cletus, Clement, and Sixtus" can sound like "Comet, Cupid, Donner, and Blitzen." The communion ought to be joyous with happy children's songs or a blessing for babies.

Thus, it becomes obvious that we must free these two basic elements—WORD and EUCHARIST—to communicate and nourish in their simplicity.

In this light we would encourage fewer verbal explanations to allow the child to experience freely, quietly, and intuitively the meaning of the action itself and its relevance to each person. Too often, we are anxious to explain every act and fill up every moment. Our liturgies become verbose, filled with a multiplicity of concepts, which, if not beyond the imagination of the child, bombard him with too many images.

Consider how many themes and subthemes occur in a typical Sunday liturgy. There is *trinity* in prayer endings, *penance* in the opening rite, *praise* in the "Glory to God," the *scriptual* theme and Father's adult sermon. After the Creed full of difficult concepts, come *bread* and *wine* and *money*, too. Then that long *eucharistic prayer* and finally, we have a familiar *Our Father* and the *peace greeting*, if it hasn't been omitted! *Communion* is only for *big* people. Hopefully, it'll be over soon so we can get down to the serious business of doughnuts and chocolate milk.

We believe it makes a lot more sense to simplify, simplify, simplify—constructing the Mass around a cultural theme that is enhanced in a penance rite, prayer, readings, homily, song, action and follow-up. The sample liturgies which follow in the second half of this book are based on these basic elements.

With such careful planning the rite should not exceed twenty to thirty-five minutes, depending on the age and size of the group. If the celebrant establishes rapport with the group or if the occasion warrants it, a longer celebration might occur. It is advisable, however, to add to the pre- or post-liturgy celebration rather than lengthen the liturgy itself.

Principle two: spontaneity in execution. Careful preparation and explanation in advance of a good liturgy are of great value. Because children learn by doing and experience is prior to awareness, physical involvement should be encouraged. Guided freedom of expression in word and gesture should be provided. There is a richness in the life experience prior to the liturgy. One might allow participants to do a "show and tell" homily or have them bring a clipping or other object to paste on a poster as part of the entrance rite.

How free are the children to sit comfortably and move about for processions, dance, communion? Desks and pews are a definite barrier to spontaneity.

Drama can allow for group sound effects that are spontaneous but orderly. Finger play and hand clapping are other excellent outlets.

As the eucharistic action heightens, the children should be free to move around the altar like teens around the bandstand of their favorite music group. Care should be taken not to allow general disorder, but neither should priest, catechist or parent become disturbed by relaxed spontaneity. The priest, especially, as a good leader, can do much to set the pace for spontaneity in children's worship. We can presume that Jesus smiled when he blessed the little children and still desires their uninhibited presence today!

Principle three: community in expression. Salvation involves the total person, individual and social. God chose to call his people together through the waters of the Red Sea. Jesus gathered his friends together to teach and celebrate on the mountainside and in people's living rooms. God still becomes most present and vital to man in the *community* gathered together for worship.

Jesus chose many communities in which to share word and food. Sometimes it was on a mountaintop with Peter, James, and John. Other times, he walked among a community of lepers or shared a meal with a tax collector. And at still other times it was small children clinging lovingly to the master's arms.

We believe he still wants to celebrate with children in community, not merely in a gathering, but in a natural and viable gathering to celebrate the community that is and to foster what it can become. At times, this might involve a single class. At times, it might be a special group such as a ball team or scout troop. Look for the times and groups: after a unit of study is finished, before an important event or game, in a time of special need, or at a joyful period of the year.

In urging such celebrations for a community of children, we do not wish to indicate that a child should be separated from the parish adult faith community at worship. Such exposure enables him to grow toward an adult expression of faith. Nor do we rule out occasional masses for the whole school, where the child can experience that he is part of a greater community of life and love.

IMPLEMENTING A PROGRAM OF CHILDREN'S WORSHIP

Now that we have discussed the principles involved in children's and youth worship, we would like to share three letters that might be used to introduce such a concept to catechists, priests and parents who form, perhaps along with a group of students themselves, the "team" that shares faith in community worship.

To the Teacher

Dear Catechist:

As you face your class of little (or big) ones for the first time, you probably share the common human situation of being "shelled," not unlike the teen's realization that he has a date on the same night with *two* of his favorite girls. Well, welcome to the human race! Incidentally, the little word "human" as we shall see, has a lot to do with catechetics and children's liturgy. Catechizing and celebrating the faith life of your children is nothing other than trying to be an authentic person and relating to your students in a deeply human way.

Let us first recognize that each of us has a basic need to feel wanted and needed—by Christ, parents, children. Your students are in need of love and understanding, of experiencing in you the fullest meaning of all that is Christ—Christ among men—the human Christ.

Basically then, your role as catechist-liturgist will involve three areas: **Life, Community, Celebration.**

Life: By this word we mean that complex of experiences—emotional, intellectual, physical (internal and external)—that have gone into making you what you are. As an adult you have already experienced a good slice of life. Your senses are keen; your ability to share life in depth, developed. Many of the ideas in today's religion texts, utilizing good psychology and pedagogy, are based on sharing the simple experiences of life—friendship, love, fatherhood, brotherhood. Consequently, you have a rich treasure of personal life experiences to open to the children around you.

Community: What we have become! Our experience of life has not been lived alone. It has developed through the influence and interaction of many groups of people, both formal and informal—the environment of mother's womb, the neighborhood playmates, the sorority, the union, the religious order. These groups have likewise helped shape your God-concept and your prayer life. Many of these groups have joined in sharing the liturgy with you. Now you have in the classroom the beginnings of a new community that will have its own style of life and growth. As you work with your class, you will become more and more involved in the life and joy of this new class-community. There will be shared experiences throughout the year—experiences in the life of the catechist and of the students—that will build this exciting new community. What a joy it will be to enter into this developmental process!

Celebration: Life and community burst out in celebration! Witness a child in a moment of intense happiness. He skips, she sings. Witness a community celebrating its life: the joy-agony of a wake, the relaxation-celebration of a vacation. These "rituals" arising out of life help us to celebrate our being and our relationship to God and one another.

As you live out the present days with your class, you will once again experience with them the joy and pain of life together that emerges into a cry, "Let's celebrate together." When this happens, it is important to remember three things: (1) Those involved have a life style and experience that they bring to the celebration. Allow the celebration to draw on this experience following the formal content or background of the occasion. (2) Allow the celebration to be something fresh and new, to grow creatively. In para-liturgical celebrations there is the greatest freedom. Even in official liturgies the accepted practice in many parishes allows much creativity. (3) If the celebration flows naturally from the life experience of the community and captures prayerfully a particular moment, it should also help the community to move back into life with a new perspective, sharing the grace of that celebration by a changed life, bringing that grace to the lives of others. "The celebration is ended. Go forth in peace to love and serve the Lord in your fellow man" is never more true than when it is carried on in living faith.

Now that you catch a glimpse of the possibilities of celebration—based on the life experience of teacher and student and aided by auxiliary materials—let us consider two other important persons involved: the priest and the parent.

The Priest: Remember his background and value systems; seek to meet him in an understanding way. Spend some time planning together with him. Spell out what is needed or desired from the priest (e.g., amount of time, manner of approach), recognizing that a negative reaction often comes from a lack of understanding of what is expected of him.

Offer to aid with insights as to how he can meet the child on his level. ("Father, this is how an adult would say it; this is how we say it in second grade.")

The Parents: Parents are very concerned about their children and communication and coresponsibility between teacher and parent are most necessary. Try to establish a line of communication from the beginning! Use the service of newsletters and parent meetings to share insights. Help parents to understand the new approaches to the concept of faith and its effect on religious education. Give them hints (perhaps already laid out in teacher-parent manuals) for celebration and growth of faith life in the home.

Lastly, dear catechists, remember as scripture says, "How beautiful are the feet of those who preach the gospel." Good luck and God speed you in your task. Be yourself; share your life and love. Celebrate! It'll be a great year.

To the Priest

Dear Father:

Every priest that I have met has a soft spot in his heart for the unfortunate, the poor, the underprivileged. Indeed this was the mark of Christ himself. Permit me to say that there is a special group of "poor" in many parishes—our young children. They are thirsting for the word of God which we try to provide for them in our religion programs. Psychology and our own experience tell us they cannot yet take the full, strong meat of adult faith. For the moment they must be drawn to Christ through personal experience and simple reflections. Consequently, they love to experience the fatherhood of God and the friendship of Jesus through persons, especially you, the priest, leader of the parish family.

It is extremely important, then, that you set aside twenty minutes or so from your busy schedule to be with these "poor." Their needs are simple. No profound words such as one might say to a terminally ill parishioner are necessary. There is no long preparation as one might give to a sermon. These children need simply to visit with you and celebrate your visit.

When adults visit they often enjoy certain rituals—a meal, cocktails, seeing home movies. So too, our children enjoy ritualizing their young experiences. We hope you can share that ritual, at least in a nonliturgical manner. As you and your children get acquainted and begin to enjoy being together, you can celebrate "officially" by using a liturgy in which the children can participate fully. Vatican II has said that "Liturgical formation should be in accord with one's age, condition, way of life, and standard of religious culture." You might arrange with the teacher for a celebration that will express the meaningful realities of who we are and what we do, offering them to God the Father within the sacrifice-oblation-meal of the mass.

So, Father, in addition to your contact with your adult parishioners, your visits and liturgies with the children are most important. Your teachers can assist you in understanding the approach to young people. But don't really "worry about what you are to say." The most important thing is that the children be able to see you as their friend and experience through you, as through all of us, the love of the Father and the person of Jesus. On the level of day-to-day experience, we all know the important role of the father and the problems that arise from fatherless homes. It should be the privilege of young students to have their "spiritual" father with them from time to time in their "classroom" home.

To the Parents

Dear Parents:

All parents naturally want to share the good things in life with their children. It is for this reason that you first brought your child to the font of baptism, shared with him your faith, and initiated him into the Christian community. It is also in this connection that you are providing for his continued sharing in the wisdom of mankind.

You have asked the teacher to share with you that process of growth and education. But for education to be truly effective it must be a team effort. Your personal experiences as a family and your understanding of the uniqueness of your child need to be joined with the training and experience of the "classroom parent," the teacher, and with the celebrations of the spiritual father and the parish family. We must reinforce each other's work. Otherwise, the value of much experience and effort will be dissipated. It is advised that you join together on occasion—father, mother, priest and teacher—to share insights and approaches. Our monthly newsletter and the myriads of "notes" that seem to infest the school-home life, as well as personal discussions, offer such opportunities.

One of the special areas of concern to all is how your child grows in his faith life. Jesus apparently had a very different approach in allowing the little children to come to him than he had with adults such as Mary and Martha, the Pharisees or the Apostles. Psychology and educational practice point out also that each stage of development in your child demands a different response, e.g., pablum for the baby, then junior foods, or simple ideas with much gesture and patient acting out until larger words and ideas can be grasped. It is the same in the process of religious education today. We continue to grow and experience our faith from an adult level. But in sharing this faith experience with our children we must be aware of their stage of development (especially regarding faith concepts).

As an added help toward understanding some of the current approaches to religious training, we would like to recommend the books: *Who, Me Teach My Child Religion*, (Curran, Mine Publications, Minneapolis, Minnesota) and *Growing Up*, (McCall, Paulist Press, New York/Paramus, N.J.) as well as the parent manual of your child's religion text.

Cooperating with the school on religion is important. Here your child has frequent opportunity to "celebrate" in the class family some of the joys of being together in Christ. But it is essential that you "celebrate" your joy and growth in Christ *at home*. For this reason we encourage you to take a look at an excellent book by Moser titled *Home Liturgies* published by Paulist Press.

May God bless your continued efforts and interest!

GENERAL GUIDELINES

INTRODUCTION

Revitalizing worship for children involves a guided freedom to experiment and make adaptations, which are relevant and expressive of their innermost being. To enable children to worship is to establish coherence of group response, to effect intergroup relatedness in Christ. To make this possible, the catechist-priest-parent-child team might use the suggestions below for putting together the elements of a creative children's liturgy.

The most effective liturgies seem to be the result of group planning. Such planning encourages a proper attitude toward the unity and participation of the persons involved. Children in the primary grades through the middle grades can well participate in the planning. On the other hand, junior and senior high students can themselves do most of the planning and development of the adaptable elements in the liturgy, from the physical arrangements to the creation of decor and visuals.

Preparation consists in bringing together the component elements in such a manner that they form a wholeness or unity. The focus of most of the elements in a liturgy is a particular phase of the child's faith development and growth. There is no need to spell out each area of life.

May we note, however, that external, adaptable elements are far from being the primary focus. Frequently the new approach to worship is referred to as the "guitar mass" which at best is inaccurate. The core of liturgy refers to the experience of worship and not to the subjective form of music-expression used by the group. What is considered most important is the spirit which the faith community brings to their God in prayer.

Because basic patterns of human life are currently more flexible than in the past, it is important that we ritualize newness of life and stress originality in patterns of worship. The newness must always emphasize that God is infinite in his creation. Whatever form our worship assumes, we must remember that God is the focal point.

THEMES

The theme chosen is central to a good liturgy. This theme may come from the liturgical year (since the key mysteries should always be celebrated). It may come from the life experience of the group members (e.g., the teen struggle for faith), from the community consciousness (e.g., Scout Week, Thanksgiving), or from the concepts developed in a catechetical program.

The overtones of the theme, expressed simply, should be integrated as often as possible into the parts of the liturgy (e.g., introductory comments, penance petitions, orations, readings, petitions of the people, offertory symbols, communion meditation, and the closing rite).

In our global community it is important to consider the needs of different ethnic groups. We should recognize the significance of having special liturgies for different ethnic groups using themes suitable for special community celebrations, e.g., a Chicano celebration for a good crop, or for someone who is moving away from the community; a black celebration for Martin Luther King's anniversary, or a Cajun (of French descent) celebration for the shrimp festival.

In selecting themes specifically for small children, it is important to recognize the real life situation and level of their growth, and relate these to their capacities and needs in worship. Six- and seven-year-old children live somewhere between illusory and real life situations which they try to concretize in that which they can see and touch. They generally experience life intuitively at a simple level during this initial development of reason. Thus, their idea of God at this point is largely restricted by human images. Taking all this into consideration, it is understandable that religious psychologists encourage simple and concretely expressed themes such as:

- personal gifts: eyes, ears, tongue, nose
- the beautiful world
- Mother and Dad
- food
- friends
- light
- water
- work and play
- experience of bread
- signs of life

A growing consciousness of the group develops as children get older. Many more activities with peers are engaged in—scouts, clubs, neighborhood and school groups. As the children develop this association with a group and a more conscious identity, they are able to relate to more abstract themes which parallel life's experiences.

Themes with a more or less direct application to their faith development could be used in the celebration of civil holidays such as Independence Day or Labor Day. The important elements in life—ecology, time, listening and choosing, discovery—can also arouse interest and meaning in worship. Themes more directly concerned with our relationship to God and others—reconciliation or forgiveness, hope, death, the prevention of drug abuse, overcoming prejudice, freedom, sharing, peace, thanksgiving, love, achieving goals at home or school—can be meaningful. These themes are statements of the values with which children are confronted outside of worship in the life situations. Thus their eucharist is a reaffirmation and celebration of that which they are trying to internalize or underwrite with their lives. (A list of approximately one hundred themes indicating the age levels of children who could relate to these themes is included in the section "Suggested Themes for Liturgies."

READINGS

God's glory is children fully alive, fully human. God's glory is also the life of the fully human person, Jesus, as shown in the scriptures. This life story has been a gauge for the Christian child in search for his identity and his faith. Unlike the generations who were exposed principally to the printed page, the children of today have been touched by radio, television and movies—a multi-media communication system with a great deal of personal interchange and some spontaneous understanding. The personal presence of the "medium as message" enables the child to sense the "believing teacher" as a modern prophet.

In order to achieve a balance in the growth of the children, it is important for the parent, teacher or priest to determine the scope of the scripture readings used at the eucharist during the year. We have been accustomed to a precise liturgical year sequence of readings. Many of the creators of good liturgies for students are now becoming aware of a real thrust toward understanding scripture in areas that used to seem irrelevant. This renewed relevance of scripture today, the way in which the word touches the lives of children, will lead planners of liturgies to be selective in the choice of meaningful readings that relate to the needs and interests of the children at any age level.

The most logical procedure in selecting a biblical reading is to determine the key idea of the theme. For example, if the celebration has the theme of brotherhood, determine which key idea of brotherhood the celebration is to highlight: service, love, friendship, or trust. However, if the reading is already set for the celebration, the theme should flow from the message of the reading.

Use one of the many library copies of the Bible Concordance, such as *Cruden's Concordance* by Alexander Cruden (Fleming H. Revell Company, Old Tappan, New Jersey) or *Concordance of the Bible* by Newton Thompson (Herder and Herder Book Company, New York, N.Y., 1943). These are a ready source of a large number of biblical readings, alphabetized under the specific theme or aspect of the theme to be celebrated. Check several readings to assess the value of each selection before choosing the one best fitted for the group.

Other resource volumes contain lists of Bible themes which cite several readings expressive of each theme given. *Themes of the Bible* by Jacque Guillet and *Bible Themes* by Thierry Maertens are two such lists. Both are available from Fides Publishers, Inc., Notre Dame, Indiana. In the event the celebration is for small children who would not readily understand the scriptural text, an alternative could be one of the many beautifully paraphrased and illustrated Bibles for children. Especially recommended are *The Children's Bible*, by J. Grispeno, Samuel Terrien and Rabbi David Wice (Golden Publishing Company, New York, 1965), *Bible for Young Christians* by A. M. Cocagnal and Rosemary Haughton (Macmillan Company, New York, 1967) and *Good News for Children* by Sheri D. Haan (Baker Book House, Grand Rapids, Michigan, 1969). There are some excellent adaptations of biblical texts in the teacher's guides accompanying the religion texts in several series.

How important it is for the liturgy team to remember that the purpose of the scripture is to show the beginning of Christianity and give children guidelines for living. A life illuminated by the Word of God is a child's response to his Father.

Isn't this sufficient to indicate the importance of God's Word? The proclamation of this work or a contemporary reading is done by a member of the community: a child, the teacher, a parent, or priest. The place occupied by this lector should be immediately before the worshipping group, rather than physically removed at a distant and elevated pulpit or lectern. To communicate effectively the significance of the message and to interpret this message is to share one's own beliefs. It is also to try to discover how God is coming to the group through this message. The whole action belongs to each one present in the effort to listen, to respond silently, and to become more fully human—like Christ.

In teaching, Christ used simple images, parables and stories which were familiar to the people of the time. Together, Jesus and his people discovered and celebrated life in both its beautiful and difficult moments. Today, we celebrate this beautiful past and at the same time make an effort to open up to the immediate experience of the present. To increase effectiveness, children can be led to see the pedagogical principle of relating their known experiences to the unknown situation with which they are getting acquainted in scripture.

To aid in discerning the plan of Christ in daily life, there is an unlimited supply of readings, in both prose and poetic form, which any leader in worship can profitably use for reinforcing and clarifying the message of the Gospel. The readings can be an excellent aid in relating the scriptural text to life situations.

Among the many contemporary readings it is important to provide a collection which can be effectively used as oral readings. Those which are meant to be read silently are not effective when read aloud. A few good examples of prose and poetry which could be helpful for students from very young through high school are suggested here. Others can be located in the bibliography.

99 Plus One by Gerard Pottebaum, Augsburg Publishing House, Minneapolis, Minn., 1971.

Jonathan Livingston Seagull, by Richard Bach, Macmillan Co., New York, N.Y., 1972.

Hope for the Flowers by Trina Paulus, Paulist/Newman Press, New York/Paramus, N.J., 1972.

The Giving Tree by Shel Silverstein, Harper and Row, New York, 1964.

The Prophet by Kahlil Gibran, Alfred A. Knopf, Publishers, New York, N.Y.

The Little Prince by Antoine de Saint Exupéry, Harcourt, Brace & World, Inc., New York, N.Y., 1943.

Please Touch by Edwin McMahon, Sheed and Ward, 475 Fifth Ave., New York, N.Y 10017.

One of the best approaches to increase the interest of children in a reading (biblical or contemporary) is to allow them to select the reading themselves. Junior and senior high school students are quite capable of making wise selections which will be representative of their understanding and needs. In this way, unexpected and unsolicited leadership can be sparked by a "multiplier" whose joy is to spread "the good news." This leadership role in worship has resulted in the development of some persons whom John Killinger describes as "sensitive, creative, grappling with the problems of being human and secular and whole in our time" (cf. *Leave It to the Spirit*, Harper & Row, New York, 1971, p. 156). A concerted effort by this kind of

Christian, anxious to form himself according to the spirit of the Gospel and to inform others of this spirit, will do much to convey the transcendent message of the transforming word of God.

PRAYERS

The major concern in constructing a liturgy is to create an atmosphere which will enable children to pray, to experience an encounter with the Father at whatever level of development they have reached. It is beyond the ability of an adult to know what happens between the Father and a particular child, no matter how reflective or how distracted the child may appear. Yet a few general norms for promoting such experiences can be suggested.

The fact that God is a person not physically seen by the child points to the need to guide the child to speak to God with other persons present. This type of prayer assumes many forms to signify the union of the worshipping group. A significant presence at the eucharist is God's presence in each person around the altar. For children to recognize the goodness, love, and support of God and others (consciously or unconsciously), is a measure of their giving and receiving Christian support—an authentic prayer form. Their faith also enables them to affirm their belief in the presence of Christ in the eucharist in prayers shared together and in silent reflection.

In terms of this deep, penetrating mystery of faith life, how are students to address the various prayers expressed at the eucharist? Generally, the *opening prayer* is a greeting, an affirmation of each other's presence and God's presence among the praying community. The usual greeting is "the Lord is with you; the grace of Christ, the love of God and the fellowship of the Holy Spirit be with you all." However, the celebrant can greet the community in a spontaneous manner as a people who need each other and who need Christ. This need is made clear in order to bring to consciousness what the children are about to celebrate.

Because the children belong to the family of man and the family of God, it is important for them to reconcile their differences in order to achieve unity. At the *purification rite* children become more aware of their need to forgive and to be forgiven. This plea for mercy and forgiveness is expressed to the community who has been offended in a variety of ways. Among some of the meaningful forms is a pause for silent reflection specifically directed to areas of life related to the theme of the eucharist. This reflection may be terminated with the Our Father or the absolution traditionally used at the eucharist and perhaps a gesture of peace.

Another variation could be short statements of behavior related to the theme for which a community may have been built. The worshipping community may use any meaningful response, as "Lord, have mercy," "Lord, I am sorry," or "I ask God and those whom I have offended to forgive me." On another occasion the children could be invited to write on a small piece of paper their greatest fault and on the reverse side the behavior which would counter this fault. Then the papers could be burned in a brazier near the altar, during the penitential rite. At eucharistic celebrations for small groups, the children may find it significant to express individually their own struggles or pleas for forgiveness.

Each form of the rite is concluded with the general absolution of the *penitential rite*. The personal involvement of each child in the communal expression of this reflective prayer will depend upon his level of understanding. It is only necessary to impress upon him that Christian faith is geared toward action and internal participation rather than spectatorship. It can then be left to him to determine the degree to which he is ready for such participation.

Prayer sometimes invites a person to assume the role of listener. This is true especially at parts of the *word service*. The most profound and relevant written source of Christian thought in human history is the word of God. Faith and reverence for this word enable the believing community to interpret the message as the ongoing process of Christian life. The Old Testament stories prepare for Christ; the New Testament authors speak directly of Christ as his friends saw him, believed him, and loved him. To enable children to expand their vision of Christ and their basic integrity, the Gospels are given a priority at the word service. To assist in guiding the development of a relationship between Christ and children is a commission to "teach" and to spread the "good news."

There are many graphic and penetrating ways of guiding children to understand the significance of Christ's hidden presence in the Gospels. The most suitable and notable element in the sharing of the word is the enthusiasm of adults for the scriptures and the values personally embodied in the persons proclaiming the word of God. This enables the dynamic process of the children's response to the word of God to be an awakening of their consciousness to the person of Jesus. The acceptance of the presence of Jesus attributed to the Gospels is not automatic, and the children's response is not necessarily immediate. It is children understanding the possibility of living out this authentic charter which enables them to say "yes" to Christ's invitation.

At the eucharist, children can respond in a spontaneous prayer which can be silent or spoken. Beautifully expressed psalm adaptations or prepared prayers can adequately affirm the "yes" of the worshipping group. Appropriate hymns or contemporary songs are frequently valuable prayer responses to God's word and a good way to communicate with God. In this manner the response concretizes the message of the Gospel to enable the worshippers to internalize it, allowing the message to become part of their lives, lives which are centered on the spirit of the Gospel rather than on the literal interpretations of each passage.

To help recapture some of the flexibility of early worship (forms of worship prior to the Council of Trent), the child should be encouraged to express his thanks, his needs, as well as those of the global community in the *prayer of the faithful*. Children who are generally dependent upon others for the satisfying physical, emotional, academic, social, and spiritual needs can frequently appreciate the needs of others. With proper guidance, these prayers can help develop among children a deep sense of interdependence among global neighbors who are big or little; poor or rich; white, red, black or yellow. This prayerful appreciation of the human family can lead children to a grateful attitude for all the gifts they enjoy, as well as a supportive attitude for those who are less fortunate than they. These prayers add relevance and freshness to any celebration shared by young children and teens. When the hopes, fears, and joys felt by the group on a personal or larger community level are spontaneously shared, a deeper sense of belonging develops.

In the *prayer over the gifts* a close bond between God and his people is expressed in gift giving. God's act of offering by sharing his love with his people of the Old and New Testaments is shown in the form of bread. When Christ taught us to pray, he asked us to say, "Give us this day our daily bread." This bread is a sign of all our needs today.

In various ways the bread was shared in the desert (Exodus 16). When Moses led the Hebrews through the desert for forty years, they were fed with manna. In John 6 we read of the boy who shared his loaves and fishes with the crowd, as Christ gave thanks and blessed the basket of food that he carried. As a sign, bread is almost universally representative of the sustenance of life. In daily life and at celebrations, every child has his own loaves and fishes—personal gifts—which he can offer to the Father through others. Gifts offered are prayers too, in the sense that they are visible signs of what the children's words denote. The prayer over the gifts should help children to focus on the action of offering the sign (bread and wine) which will be changed into a presence—Christ's presence to the children and their presence to him.

Because children have all received more than they have the capacity to give, it should be relatively easy to bring out the significance of the canon and the *eucharistic prayer.* This specific prayer of Christ provides another important moment in which the children are in a position to receive the gift of Christ's life. This is an invaluable moment to stimulate an attitude of reverence and gratitude in the recognition of so great a love—Christ's gift of himself.

During the canon the most important actions of Christ on our behalf are acclaimed: Christ has died, Christ has risen, Christ will come again. Closely linked with Christ's gift of death and resurrection is the gift of his eucharistic presence. This acclamation should be one of the key points at a celebration. It is to these peak moments that all other elements of worship should point. The wonder of Christ being present in a specific way is there to be discovered—Christ waiting, inviting each one present to share in this live-giving situation, to nourish and to be nourished. Essential to the fullest participation in any celebration is the renewed realization of the meaning of the acclamation and the reception of the body of Christ.

After receiving the eucharist children can profit by a few moments of silence in order to bring to the highest consciousness possible what it means to be one with Christ and others in an atmosphere of prayer. Special moments of life and prayer happen to each person at varying times. Therefore, it is important to provide the opportunity and foster this moment, this experience, so that a child may meet his Father and Christ, his brother.

The *communion prayer* usually recaptures the tone and spirit of the eucharistic theme and expresses praise and gratitude to the Father.

What are the mechanics which will encourage an attitude of prayer? There are as many ways to speak to God as there are persons who call to him. The simplest procedure in prayer is just to do it—to meet your Father and speak to him.

SETTING

Like the theme, the setting helps to set the tone for the community of worshippers. The setting is determined by the needs and size of the group celebrating, the occasion, and the facilities available. The church, the parish hall, the classroom, the scout house, the home, the funeral parlor, and the outdoors are the settings most frequently used. However, any place suitable for the unity and meaning of the overall liturgical action is acceptable.

Traditional church architecture often does not relate well to the needs of the children growing up in today's personalistic society.

Restructured settings make more creative use of space in relation to the persons and the worship in which they are involved. A few examples of typical settings follow.

In church
- for a total parish family celebration
- for small groups which could gather around the altar

In the classroom

In the home
- blessing a new home
- moving to a new community
- celebrating a wedding anniversary
- a First Communion mass
- a birthday
- renewal of baptismal vows of all family members

Outdoors
- a picnic in a park, near a river or lake
- a scouting trip
- a candlelight ceremony for graduation
- a family reunion
- a youth mass in a stadium

In the funeral home

In any place suitable for the unity and meaning of the overall liturgical action.

For children in a total parish family, any large area will require a setting for movement from one place to another as well as broader gestures and activities that are clearly visible from a distance. Flexibility in these enlarged movements will increase the contact which helps communication in worship. It is simply the art of using the gestures of everyday life and emphasizing them in order to make them apparent and more convincing. The physical setting for any meal at home or away from it determines in great part the cohesiveness of the group and the manner and extent of their participation. So too, at the eucharist!

The central position and height of the altar and the seating arrangement of the group are important factors. The altar should occupy a prominent space from which the celebrant is visible to everyone present. The children should be in a position nearest the altar, where they can actively participate as one group. It is important to avoid being physically scattered in a large space, because such a setting psychologically separates persons who are involved as a corporate group. Smaller groups who celebrate in a church could rearrange the seating position with chairs around the altar, allowing the children to stand around the table from the offertory through the reception of communion. In this setting, the eye movement of the celebrant is tremendously important because this helps to establish contact with the praying group. If the celebrant is deeply involved in this experience his facial expression will denote this.

The significant areas which can be designated for the penitential rite are the space in the front of the altar, the middle aisle, or the body of the church. In a very small group, individuals may be invited to express this sorrow to certain persons or to the entire group by saying for example, "I ask you to forgive me for being selfish in not showing concern for others when they were in need."

The movement to the prominent space set apart for the lectern indicates the importance of the proclamation of the word and the "good news" explained in the homily. In order to speak to children of different levels of development and different cultural backgrounds, the "good news" will have to be presented with relevant formulations of *good* and *new*.

To denote an offering representative of the group, the gifts are brought by the children from a predetermined area within the gathering. To characterize the acceptance of the bread, the wine and any other significant offering, the priest walks up to receive the offering. In each of these activities, the use of space helps convey the symbolic meaning of that action in which the worshippers are involved.

At home, the living room or den is a suitable place to participate in the *word service*; the dining room table seems to be the logical setting for the continuation of the eucharistic meal. For small children it is effective to sit on the carpet around a coffee table. Use of space, large or small, has a real bearing on the posture of the children and their facility to worship. The movements at a home eucharist or at one in the classroom can easily be seen in contrast to those performed in a large church. Eye contact, simple gestures or activities can extend the meaning of the total action. For example, at a birthday eucharistic celebration at home, the family gathers to praise God for blessing the family with each member and for enriching their lives with each one's uniqueness. Either at the beginning of the celebration, at the prayers of the faithful, or at the dialogue homily, the group could reflect on and mention a few of the God-given qualities of the person being honored on his birthday, first communion or anniversary. Prayers and petitions for the continued success of the work in which he or she is involved could be added.

In our mobile society, it is a frequent thing for a family to move into a new community. The frequency of the "moving event" in no way lessens its impact on the lives of those involved. To change communities is to withdraw a vital source of our ongoing growth and response to life. It is a withdrawal of the particular gifts a person has been giving and receiving from the present community. At the same time, it can be a rejoicing for the new possibilities in life. The possible mixed emotions—the departure from one supportive community and the anticipation of a renewed life in a new community—can be the focus of the community celebration.

A symbolic action to indicate a family's "being sent" by a Christian community might be a request, after the opening prayer, that the crucifix, the wall hangings or accessories (which are statements of what is important to the family) be wrapped and placed near the "altar table" or in a box.

Expressed at this eucharist are the thanksgiving for gifts received by this family and a plea for God's help as the family becomes part of a larger community.

Outdoors

Spring and summer are seasons which turn our attention to outdoor activities where we revel in God's creation in a variety of ways. Much time is spent vacationing, scouting, family camping, pursuing outdoor sports, and simple leisure. With these activities, there arise natural occasions, some more special than others, which lend themselves to the spirit of celebration. There are a-liturgical experiences which bring persons in touch with the deeper significance of the life-giving or life-reinforcing elements such as water, air, light, plant life, rock formations, and earth. Before a child can appreciate what these elements mean in the Christian tradition as signs of God, it is important to experience their natural significance in daily activities.

The deepening of our awareness of God as creator and sustainer is rich with possibilities of expression for children and all the members of the family.

Note how an experience of light can enrich a child's life in relation to his family's work, study, play, and worship. If a child studies the history of light and its early beginnings—the sun, moon, stars, flint stones, fire, candlelight, kerosene light, gas lights, electrical lights—he comes to realize that light is an invaluable element in his life. In scripture the image of a journey from darkness to light was used to express the feeling of freedom after a time of slavery. Later Christ is referred to as "light of the world" in a search for truth and love. Sunrise or sunset would be a beautiful and most meaningful time for an a-liturgical celebration on light. As each person lights his candle, he could point out a person or situation in which he sees the light of Christ in the world. Any family member could lead this simple celebration, which might serve as the logical basis for a eucharistic celebration on the light theme. If the celebration is outdoors, the group could be asked to walk around the area before the eucharist begins, to reflect freely on the source and development of light. In the case of an indoor celebration, the silent reflection could come after the reading of Matthew 5:1-12, "I am the light of the world."

It would also be fitting to take a common life experience—a picnic, for example—and center an outdoor liturgy expressing friendship and joy in this setting. A large picnic basket with the articles for the eucharist could be carried to the site chosen for the celebration. The setting for the word service might be under a large tree, at the foot of a huge cross made from two rustic limbs. An equally meaningful setting could be the banks of a river or lake, as Christ chose such a place to share a meal and speak with his people.

MUSIC

Music is a universal expression of any theme or mood experience by persons young or old. Used properly, music is inspirational, illuminating, and supportive of the theme on which the worship is focused. Moreover, appropriately selected music can be prayer, in the sense that songs can reaffirm the beliefs, the values and the type of life for which one is searching and praying.

Because so many of our modern songs speak so clearly of God and Christian values in the real world today, these songs often help students to express and internalize a healthy sense of reality and God.

Protest songs talk about the lack of peace, distrust, and prejudice which have to be reconciled among the people of the world. They speak of issues which confront children and adults today: communication gaps at home and away from home, social problems, political strife, injustice, hunger, and poverty at all levels. On the positive side, some songs are statements of the good for which students are searching.

This communication in song brings to a deeper level of consciousness the need for a change within children and others. However, it may be disorienting to repeat constant, negative refrains without bringing out a positive direction in which to move or alternative to choose. Any downgrading of movements, structures, or ideas should prompt a reverse current suggesting goals toward which to pray and work.

If the psyche of each person is to be immersed into the corporate activity of worship, the songs selected will need to be expressive of the group image. Today, there is an effort among creators of liturgy to consider the constituent parts of music at worship and the rationale for their use.

In this manner, music is becoming a language of social consciousness contributing to the expression of one's inner feelings.

It is important to note that among the Anglo-Saxons there has been so strong a tendency to keep emotion under control or well hidden that the full effectiveness of music has been restrained. In this age of spontaneity, there is among children a greater freedom to be more expressive.

The proper use of jazz, rock, folk rock, folk hymns, psalms, and classical music offers a wide variety of possibilities to achieve this goal. Contemporary rock, folk rock and jazz would naturally appeal to children as a vibrant expression of the movement in their lives. For the most part, these songs are a living portrait written by contemporary youth who are engaged in struggles and joys, fears and hopes similar to those of most young people. Some excellent examples of contemporary music are:

Neil Diamond, "Done Too Soon," on the album *Hot August Night* MCA-2-8000, 445 Park Ave., New York, N.Y., 1973.
Carol King, "You've Got a Friend," on the album *Tapestry*, Charles Hansen Music and Books, 1860 Broadway, New York, N.Y. 10023, 1972.
The Moody Blues, "One More Time To Live," on the album *Every Good Boy Deserves Favor*, Threshold Music Ltd., New York, N.Y., 1971.
Stevie Wonder, "You Are The Sunshine Of My Life," Stein & Van Stock, Inc. and Black Bill, Inc., ASCAP 1972.

By way of example, these few ideas about "One More Time To Live" will give you an insight into the song and its relation to life and worship. The basic theme speaks of the evolution and process of becoming more human, beginning with the frustration and continuing through the solutions. Each word seems carefully chosen to depict "confusion" as the Dark Ages in European history; "illusion" as the era of superstition in the Middle Ages; "starvation" as the expected result of believing one has all the answers, and finally, the last part of the Middle Ages when little development resulted in "stagnation." Even though much of the song explores the negative aspects of life, the overall message is one of optimism and hope.

"One More Time To Live" is similar to another song on this album: "All my life I never really knew me until today." Now I know why: "I'm just another step along the way" because of the "changes in my life." The Moody Blues conclude the first song with the significant words: "contemplation," "inspiration," and "salvation" which are the solutions to our problems because we have "One More Time To Live."

This contemporary song and so many others are filled with meaning for youth who are struggling for relevance. In another variation of modern patterns of music, Clarence Rivers encourages the fullest use of the rich black musical heritage in worship. In his album *Freeing the Spirit* (National Office of Black Catholics, 1325 Massachusetts Ave., N.W., Suite 518, Washington, D.C. 20005), there are songs which are invaluable not only for a predominately black group but also for worship in the "catholic" (universal) Church.

A question frequently asked is: Can any contemporary song be used in worship? It has been pointed out as a guideline that a song should be singable and relevant or expressive of the group's interests. The content must express positive Christian values or it must be indicated in a clear way that the negative content of a song is not acceptable moral behavior. When creative persons select songs that parallel these guidelines, it is not necessary to have a list or "index" of acceptable and non-acceptable music. The fast-paced music circuit would make this a full-time occupation.

The popular gag song, "The Cover of Rolling Stone" by Shel Silverstein (CBS, Inc., BMI, 1972), sets up materialistic values and popularity as important business. In singing "at $10,000 shows" enjoying all the "friends money can buy," the singers set their serious goal as having a picture on the "Cover of the Rolling Stone." The tragedy of this song is the exploitation of the "Blue-eyed groupies who'd do anything we say," and the false values of a group "which takes all kinds of pills for the thrills." There is one positive reference to the transcendent as they sing about "the guru; he's teaching us a better way." This type of song, derived from the conventional vocabulary of youth, is a valid expression of the wide range of human emotions and thought of a young Christian who is developing his initial faith. The thrust in the positive should be guided to more clearly expressed notions and attitudes of the transcendent. God, his love, greatness, and mercy can be recognized and validated as a great God by songs which evoke inspiration and by an image of grandeur.

Folk hymns rise from the youth cultures based on a rich Christian tradition. Musically speaking, much can be said in favor of the free forms of folk hymns which are alive, creative, and relevant. These songs are not rigidly bound to an inherited musical style but rather are fresh from the minds and hearts of youth and some adults. There is an overwhelming supply of appropriate folk hymns written and recorded for youth from preschool age through high school.

The *Hi God* album with accompanying materials is an ecumenical program based on the human growth and development for small children. Developed by Carey Landry and Carol Jean Kinghorn, the album is available from North American Liturgy Resources, 300 East McMillan Street, Cincinnati, Ohio 45219.

Another excellent resource for song and worship is the *Let Us Pray* series by Robert Heyer, Jean Marie Hiesberger and Bernadette Kenny (Paulist Press, Paramus, N.J./New York, N.Y.). These catchy songs have the freshness and spontaneity of children.

A quick glance at the bibliography and discography will give you a ready source of music in its multiforms for youth of all ages.

In view of our Jewish and Christian heritage, the great influence of sung Hebrew poetry or the psalms cannot be measured. The psalms have a poetic way of looking at the ordinary events of life and assimilating the deeper meanings, opening the imagination to greater possibilities with hope and expectance in life. Fathers Gelineau and Deiss have made a notable contribution in providing simple choral progressions to the psalms. Their translation of the psalms has provided some simple and more elaborate settings for psalms with a variety of instrumental accompaniments.

Twenty-Four Psalms by J. Gelineau, Gregorian Institute of America, 2132 Jefferson Ave., Toledo, Ohio.
Biblical Hymns and Psalms by Rev. Lucien Deiss, World Library of Sacred Music, Cincinnati, Ohio.

Psalms are primarily meant to be sung rather than spoken or read. Their purpose is to incite persons to feel what they describe. For this reason they illicit a response from the whole person, not re-restricted to an intellectual response. What deep inner joy a child can receive as he reaches out to his Father in these beautiful and traditional sung prayers, the psalms.

When it is said that much of the current music is usable in a significant manner, it is important to note that classical music also makes an important contribution in the area of worship. Well-selected classical music is excellent to accompany a reading, to provide background during a meditation, to set the tone for a celebration, or simply to be listened to prayerfully. Good examples of classical music for worship include:

Mozart's Piano Concerto, K467 in C Major, 2nd Movement
Brahm's First Symphony, 2nd Movement
Sibelius' Swan of Tuonela, any part of this composition
Chopin's Concerto No. 1, 2nd Movement
Mozart's Concerto K491 in C Minor, 2nd Movement

Pachelbel's Canon in D Major
Handel's Messiah, Behold the Lamb of God

These classical arrangements are available on many labels from almost any record shop.

Elaborate instrumentations can be effectively used for special festivals. It is important to get a balance in the length of time for music in a liturgy. Any overemphasis could detract from the worship form, rather than embellish the prayer experience. Caution also has to be exercised in avoiding an inappropriate mixture of several types of music at the same liturgy.

When the scope of musical instruments used in different Catholic cultural groups is considered, it is clear that any subjective music form ought to arise out of the milieu of that particular culture. To impose "foreign" music forms is as logical as encouraging an Indian group to use violins to accompany themselves in a rain or war dance.

In our culture, organs, piano, guitars, string instruments, combo instruments, flutes and other horns seem to be the most commonly used for worship. Yet there are other variations for blacks, Indians, and Chicanos who have their special contributions to make.

Children can very effectively sing "a cappella" or be accompanied by a piano, an organ, rhythm band, or a record. The music form most naturally suited to the group will be the most effective. In some circumstances singing a cappella will be the best thing to do—never undermining, but encouraging each voice, the God-given human musical instrument.

The experience of singing offers the possibility of expressing one's emotions and moods in prayer. Fuller participation is insured when diverse aspects of life are expressed in song hopefully and with a responsive attitude of accepting positive values and rejecting the negative. To sing to the Lord is to encounter him in songs of joy, of praise, of love.

AUDIO-VISUALS

Worship involves the total person—hence the value of visuals to enrich a person's encounter with the Father. Visuals are an effort to achieve a quality experience and to "see through" the everyday, sense-oriented world of the child. Whatever form audio-visuals assume, they are meant to make visible the invisible, to combine mystery and daily life and to show that worship is a human/divine way of seeing life and responding to it. When Christ communicated the "good news" he used images perceptible to the senses. His use of the coin of tribute, the little boy's loaves and fishes, and the scribbling in the sand were all an attempt to take the ordinary visuals of the time to relate his Father to each of us. How then did this Father choose to relate himself to his people? He did it through the person Christ, who assumed a visible human body through which man could see, hear and be "in touch" with the Father.

This "Great Prophet" is the visible sign of man's life, redemption, and salvation. All the movements of his body, his words, and his mere physical presence were a sign of hope, joy, and salvation. Through his ordinary activities of daily life, he proclaimed the Kingdom. At the wedding feast of Cana, he rejoiced with the people; at Lazarus' bier he wept, sharing deeply life's significant moments to bring out the deeper meaning of what the people saw and heard. In a personalistic reorientation to life, where we seek a deeper emphasis on social consciousness, how can life situations come alive effectively? Through pictures! Pictures speak a thousand words and at the same time allow each person to interpret the deepest meaning of the things and events pictorially represented as they relate to his own life. What a graphic way to explain succinctly the joys of family life or the pain of a drug-addicted youth through a series of "pictures." Contrast the effectiveness of radio to that of television and movies and you will get a grasp of the impact made by visuals. With the proper use of "pictures" all types of situations can be relived vividly. On the other hand, bombarding the senses with an overload of sensational audio-visuals will only entertain or distract from prayer.

A creative person, sensitive to others, will be in a position to determine what is a good balance of sight and sound for a liturgy. The extremes in blaring or scarcely heard music, or in sensational or miniature pictures, can test the endurance of any well-intentioned community. In order to achieve their purpose, visuals for children, whether in their initial or in a more mature approach to life and worship, should be concrete, simple, and expressive. It is important that children, especially the very young, be able to see, to touch, to hear, and to smell so that they can be "in touch" with life! Once children are in contact with and awed by creation, life, and people, they can more easily be guided to reach the Father.

The simple and concrete qualities of visuals often make clear an image, symbol or message that is not immediately obvious. Examples of concrete visual art forms are given below.

For teenagers a progression to more abstract forms can be employed since older children are more aware of life and its religious significance. Through the present-day multi-media educational system, many children have become geared to a diversified and accelerated process in which they can glean what "speaks" to them and filter out what is irrelevant. Such a diversity in media is aimed at reaching children of as many varied backgrounds and experiences as possible.

Participation in visuals can be started when children and/or adults initiate creative ideas, develop plans, and execute a program as sharers in reaping the enriched message. An interested person does not have to be a communication arts major to guide children in the use of the excellent supply of audio-visual materials now available in great quantity.

Where do you start or continue audio-visuals in worship for the new type of participants? It is of value for the adults who are assisting youngsters at worship to note that participants may include adherents to a variety of movements from Jesus Freaks to traditional minded worshippers. All of these youngsters will worship together in the context of a given space.

The particular area for the liturgy may facilitate the use of visuals or militate against their use. In some cases modern architects are making provisions for large wall surfaces focal to the group in order to permit viewing. Skillful use of space has also resulted in prayer rooms made from redecorated vacant classrooms. For small group liturgies children of all ages are being seated around an altar on a carpeted floor. Provisions are sometimes being made to accommodate very small groups and the use of room dividers and small screens near a low-level altar promotes cohesiveness in the group. All these settings and any other that a creative imagination suggests can be enriched by visuals created with some of the following instruments:

Projectors

- *Opaque projectors.* The beautiful color photographs or pictures in any text, or supplementary book or magazine are usually easily accessible for use on the opaque projector. A page from the Bible or a textbook or pictures from any source are slid into the machine which projects an exact reproduction in color on the screen. The pictures selected to enhance the theme could also be drawn, colored, or painted by the students from kindergarten up.

- *Overhead projectors.* Transparencies made by the children or teacher with felt pens are effective when flashed on the screen. Drawings made by the children or found in books can be reproduced by hand or machine for use on this projector. Professional transparencies are available from educational catalogues.

- *Slide projectors.* Creative persons, including those who have had little experience with visuals, can use slides in exciting and artistic programs. The visual artist has many options at his command. Slides to be used at worship can be purchased from many companies. These depict a cross-section of life situations and are readily adapted to liturgical use. Home-made ectographic slides can be sketched with color pens by the children, using blanks purchased at almost any camera shop. Life-like slides can also be made from photographs taken in the group's milieu or from pictures in books. A song accompanying the slides can easily depict the key ideas in a unified way. Another possibility is to use background music or a reading to accompany the slides.

One or more projectors can be used with one or more screens in a synchronized program. Another effective "mix" involves using two slide projectors and one 16mm projector simultaneously. The film story on the center screen carries the theme while the slides on each side illustrate other aspects of this theme as they apply to our world today.

- *Filmstrip projectors.* Biblical stories and contemporary situations to suit all ages have been colorfully reproduced on filmstrips. Caption film-strips are accompanied by a long-playing record. Or the filmstrip can be correlated with a commentary.

- *Rear projection.* Filmstrips, movies and slides can all be projected from the rear of a transparent scrim-screen. Mirrors set up at certain angles will reverse the image of the film on the screen properly. Check with the electronics experts at your local audio-visual center for details. One desirable feature of this type of projection is the fact that all the equipment and the operator are concealed behind the scrim-screen. This lessens distracting activity and frees the central position which projectors normally occupy.

Art Forms

When the very things of everyday life are used to show a child's relatedness to God, something deep within this child will develop into an attitude of reverence. It becomes an awe which says, "Today I met my God in a very real way."

Children's worship plainly shows the marks of its own time. As McLuhan has said, "Books become less our means of acquiring knowledge." It is apparent that booklike structures are being deemphasized at worship.

A setting with art forms that highlight meaningful movements, actions, and feelings is a challenge which broadens the scope of renewal at worship.

Beginning at an early age a child lives the things he does. In drawings he relives the situations he represents and the feelings of the persons and things he draws. If he creates a picture of the feeding of the multitudes, the child participates in the faith of the people who witnessed the miracle. Properly motivated, the child by his art form tells Jesus—not in words but with his whole being—that Christ is powerful and God is good in feeding the hungry. The celebrations at which childlike art forms are used become alive and vibrant, but even before the eucharist begins, the child has been enriched and stimulated. It is difficult to treat adequately in this book the limitless art forms which can be created by children and profitably employed during liturgies. However, a few examples can be given.

Working around a central theme, children through high school age can make very expressive collages, sketches, mobiles, banners, photographs, clay models, creative craft, box pyramids, home-made stoles, vestments, prayer plaques, balloons, name tags, decorated altar cloths, floral arrangements, symbolic gifts, and symbolic arrangements. In such endeavors it is important to remember that these activities are not simply meant to insure that children remember the events celebrated. They are intended chiefly to guide the child to internalize the message or deepen the truth and to give life religious value.

The use of these art forms can be indicated briefly. Simplicity and a sense of unity are key in developing creative forms. Drawings using any medium should relate to the theme and point to the message to be developed. Limitless possibilities lend themselves to the use of collages made of magazine pictures, sketches and abstract symbols. It is wise to avoid the use of highly technical creations which speak of the artist's vision of life and are unrelated to the other persons in the group. A large pyramid made of decorated boxes can make a forceful impression on a group which makes the art form come alive with their personal drawings, photographs and symbols. This creation makes a suitable background for the altar or can be placed in a position near the altar.

Balloons are a festive symbol frequently used at everything from birthday parties for tiny tots to national political conventions. An imaginative use of balloons embellishes a worship theme and sets a tone of festivity. Key words which spell out the theme can be printed on each helium-filled balloon. These are then tied a foot or two above eye level on every third or fourth pew.

By way of example, it is suggested that some of the following phrases be printed in these large balloons to be used to accompany the theme of friendship: "God is Love," "Love is not boasting," "Love is patient," "Love is kind," "Love is sharing," "Love is concern." The celebrant could expand the key idea during the homily

35

and elicit the children's understanding of and response to these words of St. John and St. Paul.

Simple actions such as each person placing his name tag on a large cross or heart hanging in front of the altar at the offertory, express a search for unity or an existing bond of unity within the group. This same bond can be manifested by a group of girls who enter the place of worship, each carrying a single flower, and place it in a container near the altar to make one beautiful arrangement. As a follow-up each flower could be presented to the mothers or teachers in an expression of gratitude.

In the case of a small group each person could sign his name on the priest's stole, made for the occasion, as they enter the place of worship. To make this possible with a minimum of difficulty, the stole and a pen are placed on a table at the entrance of the place of celebration.

An arrangement of symbols or objects placed before the altar can emphasize a theme on apostolic works. Perhaps a nurse's cap, a teacher's text, a doctor's stethoscope, a laborer's hard hat, and a cookbook would bring a deeper awareness of our interdependence in apostolic works.

Marshall McLuhan points out graphically in his book, *The Medium is the Message* (New York, Bantam Books, 1967), that the different forms of media in our society are simply extensions of persons, whether they be the psychic or physical aspects of their lives. It is vital, then, that the use of media extends the meaning of a child's life in a positive direction.

When someone asks the significance of all these visuals or these "symbols," it should be explained that these visuals point to a greater reality. They are signs or objects which embody this greater meaning and give children a thrust towards the Father. Very simply, visual symbols point to a meaning for the child which is found outside himself in a deeper life shared by God.

ACTIVITY

The act of looking or doing one thing and sensing its deeper significance is the manner and power Christ used to unite himself to persons. At the eucharist, the meaning of each thing which is said and done must be so evident that it will need only a short poetic or prayerful explanation or none at all.

In Christ's economy, no activity is too small during worship so long as it is an expression of authentic humanness. From an early age in a child's life, his frequent "why" indicates a degree of awareness that every activity or object has a purpose. Today young people are calling out for meaning, shared joy, and hope in each group activity. An endless number of purposeful activities are possible for every age and/or interest.

Processions at the entrance, offertory, communion, and recessional can involve any or all the worshipping community. There are a variety of ways and reasons in which a procession can become a significant part of worship. The persons involved, the different symbols carried and the variety of directions from which a procession moves can add spontaneity. The traditional procession can be varied by adding new participants, costumes, banners, and the like.

A great part of a child's life is spent in socializing. Therefore, any activity which can be performed together in an attitude of homage and reverence can be worthwhile. It is essential in creating liturgies that adults temporarily "put on the mind of a child." Too often adults plan liturgical activities that speak to adults rather than to children. Just as provisions are made in the classroom situation for alternate learning activities to assist each person, such accommodations are also a requirement in worship.

Because children, especially the very young, are sense-oriented, the activities must evoke a sense of worth and grandeur. A biblical or contemporary text can be used either as a simple reading or as a dramatic or choral reading to enhance its meaning. The dramatic reading is usually read by one person with great contrast in voice inflection to emphasize the content, whereas several persons perform the choral reading, executing some of the contrasting parts in unison and other parts as solo. *Murder in the Cathedral* by T. S. Eliot (Harcourt, Brace & World, Inc., New York, N.Y., 1963) is an example of a dramatic reading.

Dramatization of a theme or readings is particularly effective because of the variety of forms that the activity can assume. The use of the term drama is loosely used to include limitless possibilities for the very young as well as high school students. Beginning with simple gestures, finger plays and pantomime, young people can move up to more sophisticated participation in drama and mime.

Using children's theater to promote the glossed-over art of esthetic development is fast becoming a popular ploy. The activities in children's theater facilitate the process of self-discovery which is becoming increasingly more important to enable youth to develop an awareness of themselves and their creative power.

Possibly a brief statement about the old and new concepts of drama will stimulate adults to delve more deeply into its adaptation as an invaluable vehicle to transmit the message in the "good news." As Rev. John McCall has said, "The Gospel is not only the 'good news' but the best news we've got." Hence, the urgency to make it come alive through any reasonable media! In drama the children are the sharers of the message in the sense that the creative replaying of the gospel events enable the children to relive a meeting with Christ on the faith level.

Participation drama lends itself in an incomparable way to this type of activity. A small core of players begin to develop a biblical or contemporary story surrounded by the group of worshippers seated on the floor around them. The biblical story of the "boy with the loaves and fishes" is a likely subject choice. To prepare for the esthetic experience, a dramtic structure with thematic content is shaped by the director in advance with the core group. As the story unfolds any person in the group can participate, not only intellectually and emotionally but also verbally and physically, speaking or carrying out an activity. The purpose of this participation is to bring out a story-message from a group of children, encouraging them to create the scenes and ideas from their own experience.

In comparing the trust and generosity of the boy who shared his lunch among so many, the children express their possible response had they been present, their present response in similar situations when they are called upon to trust and to share with others. Some biblical stories are more apt to elicit participation from young children and others more appropriate for teenagers. Many of the parables or the confrontations between the gospel characters during the passion of Christ can be effectively carried out with older children.

Some valuable resource materials on drama are:
Child Drama in Action by Billi Tyas, Gage Educational Publishers Ltd., Toronto, Canada, 1971.
Participation Theater for Young Audiences by Pat Hale, New Plays for Children, Box 2181 Grand Central Station, New York, N.Y. 10017.

Mime is a distinctive art because the telling of the story, expressing the mood or emotion or describing a situation is here done without words. Every part of the body is engaged in the movements and gestures. In mime the imagination is stimulated by a given situation. The body is the instrument of expression in the role that is played. This form of communication is made up of elements that arise from the milieu in which they are performed. Mime-play is a fascinating way of communicating a story from history (biblical or nonbiblical), from everyday life, or from fantasy. Miming biblical events and their effect on everyday life is an excellent way to act out a message. The mime can be followed by a discussion; this dialogue enables children to challenge their own values and test them against the principles lived out by Christ in the scriptures.

A cursory glance at "dance" in the past indicates its importance to peoples through many centuries and of all countries. Primitive dance has a history as ancient as the Old Testament people who praised God with "drums and dancing." In primitive curing rites the shaman danced to bring about a cure. Frequently the patient himself danced as part of the treatment.

Dance for these people was an interchanging celebration of life and death situations. Through the centuries folk dances also have been a beautiful cultural expression of a way of life. In our culture however, the role of dancing or miming is more restricted whether it is associated with leisure, work, or religion.

Dance is rarely used in worship today. Its value as a symbolic manner of expressing what is important to the persons in a community is not well understood. The subtleties of the dance are still somewhat obscure because of a lack of knowledge of the "body language." In order to understand this worship form, it is also important to mention that the terms, dance and mime, cannot always be used interchangeably. Yet, they are mutually inclusive. If the general expression of mime is choreography, each movement will reinforce the content of the dance.

By way of distinguishing dance and mime it is accurate to say that the latter generally has three forms: the natural emotional expression, occupational gesture and conventional gestures. These three forms normally have more emphasis on the content. Dance is oriented to a greater degree to an expression of emotion and mood which are projected by the music or words of a song.

Dance is an art which enhances the beauty and dignity of the human body. Despite their limited liturgical use at the present time, mime and dance have been affirmed as laudable forms of worship. It is right and proper to dance a cultural and religious expression of the times as did the aborigines at the Australian Eucharistic Congress. It is a powerful and effective nonverbal way to communicate the grandeur and the struggle of life.

Some books on dance include:
Dancing for God by Deiss and Weyman, World Library of Sacred Music, 2145 Central Parkway, Cincinnati, Ohio 45214
To A Dancing God by Sam Keen, Harper and Row, New York, N.Y., 1970
Mime by Joan Lawson, Pitman Publishing Company, 2 West 45th St., New York, N.Y., 1957.

These books are just a few of the unlimited resources which will give any interested person an appreciation and methodology for teaching total body movement. As a reflection of a person's attitudes, values and human dignity, dance can reinforce the reverence and faith he has in his Creator.

SPECIFIC SUGGESTIONS

Call to Worship. The moment has arrived. All the teaching and planning for the eucharist has ended as a formal activity to allow a spirit of "let it be" and to foster the work of the Spirit in the persons celebrating.

At the outset, the call to worship should serve quickly and simply to focus attention on the theme of the eucharist and prepare the group to be open to what the eucharist is all about. This can be done in several ways:
- an introductory reading by anyone present
- a song
- mime
- a significant activity like placing a banner with the theme written on it in front of the altar
- a small representative group walking in with the Bible, handing it to each person in turn, and saying, "May the word of God help us to be better persons."
- a spontaneous prayer by the priest
- a short film strip or slides
- a dramatization or participation drama
- a collage
- an introduction of the persons who are taking part
- a short moment to reflect on why the group has assembled

Penitential Rite. In scripture Christ asked that gifts brought as offerings should be put aside until persons are reconciled. At the penitential rite Christ's mercy is offered to each person. In this context children are able to get to the core of problems of forgiveness in confronting their peers. Hopefully there will be a carry-over into the home.

At the penitential rite recognition of faults could be expressed in many ways:
- verbal acknowledgment (if the group is small and intimate)
- failures written on a piece of paper and put in a brazier to be burned
- failures written and put in one box to be elevated during the absolution
- general verbal accusations which are formulated and stated by

the celebrant and responded to by the group
- reflection on one's failures during a pause for silence followed by gestures of peace or the "Our Father."

Word Service. There are as many ways of proclaiming the word of God as there are ways to communicate to one another. Concerning the readings, it is suggested that one reading is sufficient for very small children, two for older children, possibly using one by a contemporary author.

How can God's word be most effectively proclaimed to children? The psyche and the background of the children will determine the best approach, using a combination of media which communicate the message of the Gospel rather than entertain the children. If the media are so involving that they obscure or complicate the message of the word service, change the approach.

Possible ways of restating Christ's message to the children are:
- role-playing the message in the Gospel or a contemporary reading
- dramatizing the gospel message in several different ways as mentioned above
- proclaiming the message with slides, filmstrips, movies, overhead projection of transparencies drawn by the children, dramatic or choral readings, photographs, drawings
- dialogue homily with a small group or the entire group
- essays or poetry written about the gospel message (written and read by the children)
- mime, play or dance
- a simple explanation by the priest or by a child of a large picture depicting the theme; speaking of the persons involved, their activity and the lesson taught
- several children sharing pictures of events in their lives or the lives of others which bring out the message of the Gospel
- assembling a collage or mobile to bring out the message of the reading
- dramatizing a modern song which brings out the message of the Gospel.

Offertory. Ordinarily, the offertory should be kept simple, but on occasion it may take on added solemnity and meaning. Christ used the most appropriate visual aids and symbols at the eucharist. The present-day link should be utilized.

One of the most significant preparatory actions could be the making of bread or the study of bread in its deepest symbolic meaning.

Explaining the significance of water and wine helps a child to have a reverence for the materials used at the eucharist. These natural symbols should be understood before secondary elements are added to the offertory. The life-giving qualities of water, wine and bread reinforce the greater life-giving aspect of Christ's presence among us.

Possible gift offerings which substantiate this significant part of the eucharist could be:
- an object related to theme, e.g., wheat and grapes to express the fact that though we are many (like the grains of wheat and grapes), we are one in Christ
- a flag for Independence Day
- several gifts of God for a mass on creation
- a rough cross made of two twigs for a eucharist on reconciliation
- gifts for the poor—food, clothing, toys
- a cornucopia of fruit (food for the body), a Bible (food for the mind and heart), bread and wine (food for the Spirit) for Thanksgiving
- balls and jump ropes
- books and school materials
- a baptismal or confirmation certificate for the renewal of promises
- abstract symbols or drawings expressive of peace, love, search, decision, hope
- a representative of a group walking up and making a short statement about the offering by his group
- all the objects to set up the altar could be placed on the altar at the time of the offertory
- offering an envelope with a list of all the gifts for which we are grateful
- offering our services to work for justice and equality at a eucharist to overcome prejudice
- strips of paper on which specific goals for the school year are indicated at a eucharist marking the year's beginning.

Eucharistic Prayer. Every action which has taken place up to this moment should in some way point to the mystery of the eucharist—namely, the presence of Christ on the altar and in each person participating.

In the eucharist Christ reveals fuller meanings to life and he brings about deeper relationships between persons. It is very important, therefore, to provide moments of silence, encouraging children to think their own thoughts about what is happening in this meeting with Christ. Perhaps for some, it will be a struggle for faith or a momentary search to reflect on what the eucharist is all about.

Silence can be more effective than imposing "canned" prayers or other reflections because silence can create an atmosphere apt to bring out one's own thoughts. This active internal participation can serve as the basis for an attraction to the person of Christ; hopefully, this attraction in turn would serve to modify the behavior.

Usually Canon II is used, due to its brevity, but it is quite possible that adaptations be allowed in some areas. To fail to do this—to use prayers totally unrelated to a child's experience—is an example of our failure to respect the human person. This seems to be what the creators of Vatican II's documents meant when they asked pastors "to promote active participation in the liturgy both internally and externally. . . ." With much wisdom they also state that "the *age* and *condition* of their way of life and the degree of religious culture should be taken into account" (cf. Paragraph 19). This is precisely what this book is all about! Canons adapted by the editors are included in the sample liturgies. The new sacramentary and "experimental" type liturgy books give other possibilities.

Sharing the Sacrifice. Shared faith, realized on a personal and communal level at the breaking of the bread, ought to be an experience of intense unification for the family of God. The attitude with which a child encounters Christ will flow out to others present at the eucharist.

Life and community burst out in celebration in the unity of persons who believe in Christ's presence among them. Communion under both species (wine, however, is sometimes not pleasant tasting to small children), passing the plate around, joyful processions, or sitting in a small group at a dinner table are some possibilities of variety.

Closing Rite. To have worshipped together is to have experienced something a bit different from our everyday style of conversing and sharing. The celebrant's final blessing is a prayer that we may "put on the life of Christ" as prayed for and celebrated. The blessing assumes the form of a hope or wish that our lives as Christians will be lived at a deeper level. It is often good to have a post-communion reflection and suggestions for relating the celebration to future life. Rather than ending, the mass is just beginning when we dismiss the assembled community.

"Follow-up." To "do one's thing off the cuff" without the procedure above or other well-defined plans can prove disastrous. Much research about life and worship is indispensable before adaptations can be made. Once a liturgy has been completed, an evaluation of the celebration will help to refocus on the essentials. To do this effectively doesn't require an expert with a Ph.D. in liturgy, but rather a genuine Christian who has put on the mind of Christ.

To enrich the experience of the student it is suggested that some added synthesis, celebration or project be used to extend the theme back into life. It could be as simple as sharing the flowers on the altar with shut-ins or as elaborate as organizing a recycling project for the neighborhood.

Thus liturgy arises out of life, celebrates the moment and moves prayerfully back into activity that is part of the ebb and flow of life.

Why a Planning Sheet? One of the major factors in planning a good liturgy is to determine the goal and the priorities at the outset. To constitute a eucharistic celebration some elements are absolutely indispensable, while others can be secondary. In creating an authentic experience, it is essential that the greater emphasis be placed upon the component elements of the eucharistic celebration. The proclamation of the Word, the Offertory, the Consecration, the Acclamation and the Communion are some of these essential elements.

To accentuate these significant areas, a planning sheet may be used to facilitate a proper balance. The utility of the planning sheet depends on the creativity of the persons shaping the liturgy, since it is only one of several possible approaches. For example, the theme and readings cannot be switched if there is a fixed reading. In this situation, the theme would flow from the reading rather than vice versa.

The arrangement of the different elements on the planning sheet does not indicate order of significance. The sheet attempts to insure balance and proper emphasis in the planning procedure and worship experience. The sample below may serve as a model check list for planning a liturgy. Additional points may be inserted as dictated by experience.

PLANNING SHEET FOR A EUCHARIST

I. Group _____ Occasion and/or date _____
II. Theme _____ Celebrant _____
III. Readings:
- Commentator _____
- Introductory reading _____
- Second reading _____
  (biblical or contemporary)
- Gospel _____

IV. Prayers:
- Entrance or introduction _____
- Purification rite _____
  (Our Father and Kiss of Peace can be used here)
- Response after reading (read or sung) _____
- Prayers of the faithful
- Spontaneous ___ • Assigned ___ • Celebrant _____
- Prayer over the gifts _____
- Our Father and Kiss of Peace _____
- Prayer after communion (silent, read, or sung) _____
- Canon: I, II, III, IV, or an adaptation _____

V. Music
- Song leader _____
- Type of music _____
- Songs: _____
  - Entrance _____
  - Response after readings _____
  - Offertory _____
  - Communion _____
  - Acclamation _____
  - Communion meditation _____
  - Closing song _____
  - Any other _____

VI. Activity
- Servers' activity _____

- Processions _____
- Dramatizations _____
- Dramatic readings _____
- Participation drama _____
- Slides, movies, filmstrips _____
- Dialogue _____
- Any visual, verbal or non-verbal activity
- Mime, play or mime dance _____

VII. Types of decor
- Arrangement of the altar (focal point of activity) _____
- Flowers _____
- Banners _____
- Collages, photographs _____
- Posters, letters _____
- Any creative type of decor which enhances the setting rather than distracts _____

Some specific ideas include:
- Pyramid of boxes with pictures pasted on the sides
- A wall of boxes with negative phrases on one side, rebuilt as a bridge with positive phrases written on the other side
- Balloons with key words written on them
- Mobiles
- Cards or gifts taped or placed around the altar
- Pennants of contemporary expressions
- Arrangements of objects or symbols expressive of the theme.

The following are the usual responses used at the Eucharist:
Priest: The Lord be with you.
Response: And also with you.

After the first reading:
Priest: This is the word of the Lord.
Response: Thanks be to God.

After the Gospel:
Priest: This is the Gospel of the Lord.
Response: Praise to you, Lord Jesus Christ.

Priest: Pray, brethren . . .
Response: May the Lord accept the sacrifice at your hands for the praise and glory of his name, for our good, and the good of all his church.

Priest: Lift up your hearts.

Response: We lift them up to the Lord.
Priest: Let us give thanks and praise.

Holy, holy, holy Lord, God of power and might, heaven and earth are full of your glory. Hosanna in the highest. Blessed is he who comes in the name of the Lord. Hosanna in the highest.

Acclamation: Christ has died, Christ is risen, Christ will come again.

Lord, I am not worthy to receive you, but only say the word and I shall be healed.

SAMPLE LITURGIES
SUITABLE FOR PRIMARY GRADES

Life Themes:
- Creation: Our Beautiful World
- Good Example: Follow the Leader
- Festival: Thanksgiving

Liturgical Themes:
- Church Year: Christmas
- Sacraments: First Eucharist

CREATION: OUR BEAUTIFUL WORLD

Theme: Primary children have a special sense of wonder at the beauty of creation—the variety of autumn colors, the distance of the stars. This liturgy celebrates the joy of creation and praises the designer of nature.

Materials (select or adapt the following suggestions for your group):
- Have each child prepare a small box with pictures of creation pasted on its exterior. The boxes are then stacked in a pyramid form at the beginning of the liturgy.
- Prepare a mobile with pictures of the beauties of creation and hang near or above the altar.
- Nature slides and/or children's drawings may be prepared and shown as an introduction, as a homily, or as a communion meditation.
- Pictures of beautiful scenes are taped to helium-filled balloons and carried in procession and affixed to hooks behind the altar, forming a backdrop for the liturgy. They may also be taped to the end of every third pew.
- Have the children paste treasures from a nature walk onto poster board and use as decor.
- An especially effective setting might be a beautiful picnic area. A simulated environment could also be created (see Tree House experiments in *Pace* by Gerald Pottelbaum).
- The local Jaycee Chapter may have posters on the "Pitch In To Clean Up America" Campaign.

Celebration entrance: If the visuals listed above are used, the children could take part in a procession during the entrance song.
- "All the Earth Proclaim the Lord" (Deiss, World Library of Sacred Music)
- "The Tree Song" (Robert Blue, FEL)
- "Shout from the Highest Mountain" (Ray Repp, FEL)
- "America the Beautiful"

Greeting: We are happy when we see all the beautiful things in God's creation: tall trees, lovely flowers, pretty birds, animals, the mountains, the lakes and rivers, houses and food. But the most important of all God's gifts is people because they can enjoy all the good things God has given us.

God gave us these gifts because he loves us. He wants us to share his love by using these gifts to help others. Today we think about two very special gifts: wheat to make good bread and grapes to make wine. The bread and wine which we will see today are special signs that Jesus our brother loves us and is with us.

Penitential rite: Sometimes we have forgotten to take care of our beautiful world. Let us tell God our Father that we are sorry.

For carelessly throwing trash all over our beautiful world we say, Lord have mercy.

For the way we hurt people in our beautiful world we say, Christ have mercy.

For the times we forgot to say thank you God for our beautiful world we say, Lord have mercy.

Opening prayer: Let's be quiet for a minute and think of something special to say to God our Father to thank him for the beautiful world in which we live.

Reading I: "God Made the World" (Pottelbaum, LP, G. Pflaum Co., Dayton, Ohio) or any similar reading. Use gestures to communicate the grandeur of creation and to give a religious message in a simple spontaneous form.

Scripture reading: Genesis 1:1-2, 14-22.

Homily:
- See the beauty of creation.
- Man is the most beautiful of God's creatures.
- Man is the caretaker of creation.

Another possibility is to stage a role-playing situation illustrating the reverent use of God's creatures (e.g., watering, picking and arranging flowers; taking a hike or a fishing trip in the mountains).

Prayer of the faithful: Father, out of love, you gave us your world to use and enjoy. Thank you for all the big and little things: a squirrel, a leaf, a mailbox, a refrigerator, the stars, a dandelion, the newspaper, my neighbor, weeds, and rain. This is your world, Lord. Help me to see you in all of creation

Moving in procession with gifts of wheat and grapes, wine,

bread, flowers, water and candles, the children sing: "Glory to God" (C. Rivers, World Library of Sacred Music) or "All That We Have" (Dameans, FEL).

Prayer over the gifts: Father we thank you for the wheat for this bread. We thank you for the grapes in this wine. We thank you for the people who helped to make this bread and wine. Help us remember to use your gifts carefully and keep our world beautiful. We ask this in Jesus' name. Amen.

Preface and canon: Father, it is good for us to thank you for your gifts. You have given us many persons and things to help us to know you better. These gifts, both great and small show us how much you love us. For all this we say Holy, Holy, Holy, Lord God of all creation. Heaven and earth are filled with signs of you and your love. We praise you for coming to us.

Priest: The Lord lives in you, children, so we will lift up our minds and hearts and speak to him.

Canon: We thank you, Lord, for the many signs that show us you are Father of us all. You sent your Son, Jesus, and your Spirit to live among us. You made food for the hungry and water for the thirsty. You gave us the sun for light and heat and to help plants grow. We thank you for all this love.

On the night before you died you invited your friends, the apostles, to share a meal with you. You took bread into your hands and thanked your Father. Giving this bread to the Apostles, you said, "Take this, all of you, and eat it. This is my Body which is given for you."

Then you took the cup, said a prayer of thanksgiving over it and said, "Take this and drink. This is the cup of my Blood. Whenever you drink this it is in memory of me."

Father, we offer you Jesus, your son and our brother. With him we want to give ourselves to you. Give us your Spirit of life. As we share this meal, teach us to live as your children. We pray for the people all over the world that they will know and love you. We praise you, Father, your son Jesus and the Holy Spirit today and forever.

Communion rite:

Song: "Bread You Have Given Us" (Wise, World Library of Sacred Music)

Response: God our Father gives us good gifts. Besides our beautiful world, he gives us Jesus as our brother in the holy eucharist. We thank him for this gift by bringing thanks and joy in Jesus' name to all the world. Let's begin by wishing a happy day to each other (greeting of peace).

Prayer: Father, thank you for the things you give us—for pencils and trees, for clouds and ice cream. Thank you for all of us—for Joe, Judy, Marilyn and Michael—and all boys and girls. But thank you especially for Jesus, our brother, who is with you, our Father. Amen.

Dismissal: Let us go with happy faces because today we have celebrated the beautiful things God has created for us to use and enjoy. As happy and holy people we live for God our Father and our brother Jesus, Amen.

Closing song:

- "Clap Your Hands" (Repp, FEL)
- "This Little Light of Mine" (traditional)
- "Come Out" (Miffleton, World Library of Sacred Music)
- "New Creation" (Dameans, FEL)

Follow-up: The posters and other decorations could be brought to a nursing home or a children's ward. Ask the pastor to let you decorate the church vestibule with "creations" for the next Sunday. The children might also plant seeds, plants, or a tree.

Let the class clean up the playground at recess and award scenic travel posters to the most diligent workers.

GOOD EXAMPLE: FOLLOW THE LEADER

Theme: Most little children love to play "follow the leader." They quickly learn to imitate grownups and play "house." Learning about Jesus as our brother gives us an opportunity to celebrate his leadership and begin our own efforts to show others the joy of following Jesus, our leader.

Materials and preparation:

- The focal point of the worship area might be two pots—one with a dead branch and one with a thriving green plant, such as ivy.
- Each child might prepare two pictures—one showing an adult doing something good, (e.g., Jesus feeding 5,000, Mother serving meals), and the other picture of themselves or another child doing something similar (e.g., sharing candy). These could be pasted on cardboard and placed in front of the altar.
- Make a large banner illustrating Jesus washing the apostles' feet. Use a caption such as "Let us follow his example and serve each other" or "He was sent to serve." Hang the banner near the altar. Surround it with the children's pictures and another caption, "We are sent to serve."
- The procession in may be a "follow the leader" type movement round the yard, up and down several aisles to a joyful tune or rhythm band (pied piper fashion).
- A collage of community leaders—mayor, bishop, policeman, parents, PTA chairman, welfare worker may be displayed.
- Slides showing children working and playing together, used with a commentary, would provide a homily or meditation.
- Each child could draw and cut out an outline of his feet. These are taped to the wall following behind a symbol for Christ.

Celebration introduction: Before our country was filled with highways and buildings it was a forest of trees. Brave men led pioneers out to clear the forest, plant crops, and build roads. They were leaders.

Sometimes the people wouldn't help one another or work together. All men need good leaders to guide them to love and work with each other. There is a leader whom God sent to help us build love between men. He is our brother Jesus. Today Jesus is represented by his friend Father _____. Let us follow him and sing.

Entrance song:

- "Here We Are" (Repp, FEL)
- "Come Out" (Miffleton, World Library of Sacred Music)

Greeting: Yes, Jesus is our leader. We are glad he called us at baptism to be his people, his brothers and sisters.

Penitential rite: But sometimes we don't follow Jesus. Sometimes we don't love each other. Let's think about those times and tell Jesus we are sorry.

All: I confess to God my Father, to Jesus my brother, to his friends and especially to you, my classmates, that I have not been a good follower of Jesus. Sometimes I have been selfish and thoughtless. And so I ask all of you and especially Jesus, to forgive me. Amen.

Priest: May God and our brother Jesus have mercy on you, forgive you and help you to be a good follower.

Response: Amen.

Opening prayer: Father, Jesus followed your plans, was obedient to his parents and followed their example to help make this a better world. Help us to follow Jesus and give us your Spirit to do our best to help others too. Amen.

Reading I: John 10:1-16 (Jesus, the Good Shepherd). An alternative response might be a simple adaptation of Psalm 28.

Priest: Lord, what kind of person do you like? Is it the child who does not fight with his brothers and sisters, who does not talk about his friends and takes good examples from those who do good? Yes Lord, but we also know that these things are not easy. We know that you love the person who tries, who wants to choose what is right and who calls to you for help.

Reading II *(Suggestions):*

- Jesus feeds the 5,000—Matthew 14:13-21; Mark 6:30-44; Luke 9:10-17; John 6:1-14.

- "I am the true vine"—John 15:1-10.

Homily: Jesus uses us as we are. We do the best we can and offer what we are. Through us Jesus can do great things. OR discuss the meaning of a vine—to grow and to cooperate.

Offertory song: "Whatsoever You Do" (Jabusch, ACTA). Pantomine the various images, e.g., hungry children—hands on stomach.

Prayer over gifts: Father, you give us bakers to make our bread. You give us farmers to grow grapes for our wine. You help us to work together under our leaders to make this a good world. Strengthen us in your Spirit through these gifts that Jesus may be our leader. Amen.

Preface and eucharistic prayer: Father, it is right and good that we should say thank you. We thank you especially for Jesus, our leader and brother. He came to teach us; he came to save us. He died and rose again and is with you. Now he sends his Spirit to be with us. We join together to thank and praise you as we say (sing): Holy, holy, holy Lord God of all. Heaven and earth are filled with your glory. Hosanna in the highest. Blessed is he who comes in the name of the Lord. Hosanna in the highest.

We thank you, God our Father, for sending your son Jesus to live with us. He fed the hungry. He gave drink to the thirsty people. He healed the sick and showed us that you love us.

We thank you for the love that he gives us. On the night before he died he called his friends together and told them that he wanted to share a meal with them. He took bread into his hands and thanked you, his Father for all that you had done. Then he gave the bread to his friends and said to them. "Take this, all of you, and eat it. This is my Body, which is to be given for you." Then he took the cup, said a prayer of thanksgiving over it and told his friends, "Take this and drink. This is the cup of my Blood, the Blood of the new and everlasting life which will be shed for you and for all with forgiveness and love. Whenever you do this, you will do it to remember Jesus."

O Lord, we remember all that your son did for us. He died for us; he came back to life and went up to be with you in heaven. But Jesus still lives with us.

Father, we ask that you send the Holy Spirit to us so that we may really be friends of Jesus and leaders to all we meet. We pray that we may live as you have asked us and that we may serve all those who need us.

This we ask with all men who believe in you. We pray that we may always be children of God—the church of Jesus. Through Jesus and with Jesus and in Jesus, we praise you, our Father with the Holy Spirit, today and always. Amen.

Let us now take the example of Jesus and pray to our Father, asking him for the things that will help us to be better children in his family. (For a small group mass, the children can make a circle around the altar and hold hands as a sign of friendship while they recite the "Our Father").

Prayer before communion: Lord Jesus, the food which you are giving me is your own Body and Blood. It is the true Bread of Life and love. You are giving me this special food of love so that I may be an example to other children as I live, work and play with them. Help me to be a leader for you, Jesus.

Communion song: "They'll Know We Are Christians" (Schalte, FEL).

Prayer after communion:

Priest: Let us think quietly (for one minute) of some good actions which Jesus and our parents have done to give us a good example to follow.

Response: Father in heaven, we thank you. May the holy food we have received give us the strength to live as real Christians at home, at school, and wherever we go.

Priest: We have said thank you to Jesus for being our leader and telling us about the Father's love. Let us remember to say "thank you" to others who lead us and help us to know the Father's love. We will prepare a little gift to bring to them.

Final blessing:

Priest: Go now and take Christ with you.
All: We will go into the world and be examples to other children.

Recessional hymn: "Witness Song" (Blue, FEL).

Follow-up: Have the children deliver a little gift to some leader, e.g., principal, lunchroom supervisor, parents, crossing guard, pastor, fire chief or police chief.

FESTIVALS: THANKSGIVING

Theme: "Thank you" is a phrase which is part of our everyday life from early childhood up through adult life. This liturgy celebrates our remembering to say thanks for our blessings.

Materials and preparation:

- A beautiful outdoor setting would lend itself to this celebration. A variety of natural elements could surround the altar or be placed underneath it (e.g., pumpkins, sugar cane, fall leaves).
- Have the children write thank you notes to people who offer their services to the children. These could be presented at the offertory and mailed or hand delivered after the liturgy.
- Slides assembled by the teacher, sound filmstrips or a short movie might be shown (e.g., "Sky," 16mm film, National Film Board of Canada, Regional Office, Mackenzie Bldg., 1 Lombard St., Toronto, Canada).
- Have the children start a collection entitled "We Are Thankful for the Smallest Things." Include such items as seeds, tiny shells, a tundra flower, pebbles.
- The latest-born baby from among the families in the group (or from a poverty family) could be brought to the liturgy and honored with a gift from the group.
- Each child should make a list of the ten things for which he is the most grateful. The lists could be given to the priest at the offertory.
- Set one long table in the school cafeteria. Cover with a bright tablecloth and place a candlelabra and a cornucopia on either end. A loaf of bread and a bottle of wine are placed in the center of the altar. At the offertory each child places one piece of fruit on the table. A tiny thank you note to God can be taped to each piece of fruit before it is presented.

Celebration introduction: Did you ever stop to think about a tiny lady bug? The lady bug helps us by eating insects which harm our plants. Did you ever see a contact lens? It is so very small. But it helps us to see and read and learn. There are so many little things that we can say thank you for. And there are many big things too. Can you name some of the big things we are thankful for? (Allow children to respond.) There are so many things to be thankful for. Let's learn to sing our thanks.

Entrance song: "Good News" by Mary Lou Walker (*Songs for Young Children*, Paulist Press).

Opening prayer: Jesus, our brother, you sat down to talk and to eat with your friends. You always reminded them to say thanks. We want to say thank you too, so we've come together today to celebrate. Amen.

Reading I: Eccl. 4:1-10.

Response: Show a film or slides of things we are thankful for.

Reading II:

- Luke 17:11-19 (the ten lepers), or
- Mark 8:19 (dramatize).

Homily: There are many important things, important people, important dates but we forget them so easily. We should try each day to thank Jesus for all he did and ask for help in remembering to show our thanks to others too.
During the homily it is important to emphasize the message—Christ is showing us how to live. Personal experiences of the children, expressing their gratitude to others and to God should be shared. These experiences should be very simple because Christian living is a life of trying to live more deeply the simple events.

Prayer of the faithful: Response: Thank you, O Lord, thank you.
We say thanks for the seed which grows into our food . . .
We say thanks for the rain which gives us water to drink . . .
We say thanks for the people who made the clothes we wear . . .
We say thanks for the people who keep us safe from harm . . .
We say thanks for the birds who sing such happy songs . . .
We say thanks, dear Lord, we say thanks to you.

Offertory:

- Sing "Of My Hands" (Repp, FEL) using pantomime (e.g.," . . . of my hands. . ." outstretched hands, ". . . heart. . ." arms crossed over heart, ". . . life. . ." arms stretched over head. *OR*

● *Priest:* The only place where God's word can grow is in the hearts of those who hear his word with joy. Let us thank God for the gift of his word. *(Children sit in a circle and say the responses with gestures. They begin with folded hands.)*

Priest: For the gift of food for our bodies... *(sweeping movement from head to toe toward body).*
Children: Jesus, we thank you. *(arms raised upward).*

Priest: For our Christian homes, parents and friends... *(hand in gesture pointing to friends).*
Children: Jesus we thank you *(arms raised upward).*

Priest: For all persons, animals and things which help us to know and love God more... *(both hands extend to sides).*
Children: Jesus, we thank you *(arms raised upward).*

Priest: For your life and love which never end... *(arms crossed on chest).*
Children: Jesus, we thank you. *(Children stand, skip or dance around the Bible, singing)* Glory to God, glory. O praise him, alleluia. Glory to God, glory. O praise the name of the Lord.

Offertory prayer: We thank you, Father, for this gift of bread made from tiny grains of wheat by workers who baked it with love. We pray that it will become our special food. We thank you, Father, for this cup of wine. Once it was ripe grapes and people worked hard to make the wine and bring it to us. May Jesus make it a special drink.

Prayer over gifts: Father, we see these gifts of bread and wine but we want to remember those who made them and those who helped pay for them. We especially say thank you that we are here to share as Jesus makes them a special gift of his Body and Blood for us. Amen.

Eucharistic prayer: Father, we say thank you again and again. Thanks for all your gifts and especially for your son, Jesus. He came to teach us and he gave himself on the cross for us. We ask him to send his Spirit to join us today.

God our Father, in his loving kindness sent his son Jesus Christ to be our brother. The more we see things and places and persons with love as Jesus does, the closer we grow in friendship with him. True friends in the family of God love each other and always try to live and act in such a way as to remain friends. Let's share our friendship with each other and say the words that Jesus our friend and brother taught us. *(Kiss of Peace followed by the Our Father.)*

God sent Jesus to give us the help we need to live in the family of God, the Church. On the day of baptism, Jesus called each of us to be his very special friend. Jesus died for us so that we might be friends of God. He came back to life so he could always be with us helping us to love the Father and each other even more. At the Last Supper Jesus took bread. He gave thanks to his Father. Then he broke the bread and gave it to his friends and said: "Take this and eat it, all of you. This is my Body." Then he took the cup of wine. Again he gave thanks, gave the cup to his friends and said, "Take this and drink from it, all of you. This is the cup of my Blood. Whenever you do this, you will do it to remember me."

All the good things which Jesus has done for us in the past are signs that he will always be with us. We believe that Christ died, came back to life and that Christ will come again.

Song: "Yes, Amen" (Joe Wise, FEL).

Father, with Jesus we want to give ourselves to you. Bless us and our eucharist with your spirit of love. As we share this supper teach us to live as your children. All praise and glory is yours, with Christ and the Holy Spirit today and forever. Amen.

Communion rite:

Song: "Glory to God" (Rivers, World Library of Sacred Music) or "Kumbaya" (Traditional).

Response: A good way to thank God our Father and Jesus our brother is to live as children of love and remember to thank those who help us. We might say thank you in a special way, or maybe bring a thank you note or make a small thank you gift.

Priest: Let's be quiet for a minute and think about all the people, places and things—big and small—for which we want to thank God.

Distribution of holy communion:

Priest: The Body of Christ.
Child: I believe.

Hymn during communion: "Let Us Break Bread Together" (traditional).

Prayer of thanksgiving: (The celebrant makes a request that all pause to thank God silently, in the manner below or as he chooses.)

Priest: Jesus is with us in a special way now. Let us stop for a few moments to thank him for coming to us just to show us how much he loves us. (*Pause*) Jesus will give us help to choose what is right. Let us thank him for being so kind and helpful. (*Pause*) Thank you Jesus for being a friend to each one of us.

Blessing:

Priest: Go, children, and speak of Christ to others.
All: We are happy to bring this joy to our friends.

Children walk around after holding hands and singing "Shout Out" (Witness Song).

Dismissal: Let us go out now with happy faces to thank others in Jesus' name. Thanks be to God.

Closing song: "This Land Is Your Land"

Follow-up: Have the children trace or write thank you notes; fold them and decorate with a bright seal. Then they can deliver them to someone to whom they are especially grateful. Also ask them to give a pledge of service at home as a thank you to their parents.

CHRISTMAS: JESUS IS FOR GIVING

Theme: Christmas is naturally an exciting time when children expect to be on the receiving end. As Christians, we want to teach that it is more blessed to give than to receive. This liturgy emphasizes the joy of giving in the shared song presentation, shared offertory gifts and in the post-celebration party.

Materials and preparation:
- A choir can prepare three or four carols ahead of time and invite the participants to listen and sing along.
- Each person should be asked to bring a small, wrapped gift to be brought up at the offertory and later shared with the poor.
- Punch and cookies, peppermint canes, etc. can be prepared for a party after the liturgy.
- Slides or illustrations from the book *The Giving Tree* (Shel Silverstein, Random House) and/or the Christmas story from the *Children's Bible* (Liturgical Press) are effective readings.
- Have each child draw another's profile (life size) on brown paper. Have half of the children lie on their right sides, other half on their left sides. Line the silhouettes up on either side of a large nativity reproduction as though they were the wise men bringing gifts.

Celebration introduction: Long ago, people had no Christmas. God our Father had promised a savior, but he did not come until God sent us his own son Jesus to live with us on earth. Jesus is our brother and the colorful gifts and bright lights of Christmas are to remind us of our brother's birth.

Entrance: Have a brief concert as the children sing traditional carols: "Away in a Manger," "Hark, the Herald Angels Sing," "Silent Night" (*all join in on the third verse*).

Reading I: Using an opaque projector show slides of *The Giving Tree* while the story is being read.

Response: Ps. 25: 4-5, 6-7, 8-9.
Teach me your ways, O Lord.

Reading II: Luke 2:1-14.

Homily: God the Father shared the greatest gift of all, his son Jesus. Let us think about all the gifts we have received in the past and how we must share them with others. Today we will share small gifts with the poor, but how can we share a part of ourselves everyday with others?

Prayer of the faithful: Jesus is a special gift the Father gave to all of us the first Christmas. Jesus wants to bring our prayers and needs to his Father. Let us talk to him.

Response: Jesus, help us.

That Jesus will bless the work of those who are grown-ups and have to do many important things—_____, our Pope, _____, our President, _____, our Bishop and all of our parents, we pray . . .

That those who don't know about Jesus may have people to teach them the good news, we pray . . .

That the Father will know by our happy faces how glad we are that he sent Jesus to be our brother, we pray . . .

That those who are hungry and sad may have friends to help them, we pray . . .

That we all may learn to share, we pray . . .

Offertory: For our offering let us sing "Happy Birthday" to Jesus. (If gifts have been prepared there should be a procession to place the offerings in an empty crib or at the foot of the crib.) Follow with "O Come All Ye Faithful."

Prayer over gifts: All these gifts and all that we are, we now offer with this bread and wine. Take them and unite us with Jesus and his love. We ask this of you, Father, in your Spirit. Amen.

Eucharistic prayer: Father, we praise you. We thank you for sending Jesus to us. He was born in Bethlehem. He taught us about you and told us of your great love for us. Send your spirit to help us praise you by our actions as we join in saying:

Holy, holy, holy, Lord God of all living. Heaven and Earth are filled with your joy. We praise your name. We praise Jesus who came from you to teach us.

Father, you are so kind to your children. You gave us the gift of life. You gave us Jesus as our light when he came to earth and was born in Bethlehem. Now bless these gifts of bread and wine that Jesus may come to us again in them. We remember that the night before he died he held bread in his hands and thanked you, Father. He gave the bread to his friends and said, "Eat this. It is my Body which I will give up for you." And after supper he took the cup of wine in his hands and thanked you. He handed the cup to his friends and said, "All of you drink this. Here is my Blood which is gladly given for you because you are my friends." Father, we no longer offer bread and wine but now the body and blood of Jesus our brother. We want to offer ourselves and all men—babies and grandparents, Americans and Africans, those living and our friends who have died. Bless us and these gifts with your Spirit of love. As we share this supper teach us to live as brothers and sisters with Jesus our brother. All glory and honor is yours through Jesus in the unity of the Spirit forever and ever. Amen.

Communion rite:

Song: Play background music (or record) of traditional carols. If you are celebrating with children who have not yet made their first communion, invite them to come forward and sign their foreheads with a cross.

Response: Jesus came a long time ago in Bethlehem to be our brother. He wants us to live as his friends and friends of one another. Let's take a minute then to tell each other "Merry Christmas."

Prayer: Jesus, you really do bring joy to the world by your Body and Blood in holy communion. Help us also to bring joy to others by our lives. Amen.

Dismissal: Let's go out from here now to bring the joy of Jesus to the world. Thanks be to God.

Closing song: "Go Tell It On The Mountain" (traditional).

Follow-up: The celebration should flow over into a simple cookies and punch party. Older children could go with an adult to deliver the presents collected or help pack them for mailing.

EUCHARIST: CELEBRATION OF FIRST COMMUNION

Theme: This liturgy is geared to an individual or very small group setting for First Communion in a home liturgy or small chapel. It centers around the Christian community by emphasis on family and connects the sacrament of eucharist with baptism.

Materials and preparation:
- The Paschal candle shares a place of honor and individual candles (with holders) are prepared for each child.
- Other materials prepared have a direct relationship to the eucharist. Parents, with the child's help, may bake the hosts for the mass. They can prepare and bring up in the offertory procession, the cruets and ciborium.
- The occasion should be fittingly celebrated with a festive meal at home or at a restaurant. This could add to the memory of the occasion by stressing the "food" aspect without the tendency to make it memorable by a deluge of material things and/or money.
- Songs selected should be the child's favorites.

Setting: This option could be used for one child or several first communicants in a family setting. In the case of one child, the ceremony begins with the short introductory reading by an older brother or sister or other relative of the child.

Celebration introduction: Today is a special day for each of us. At baptism we began to belong to God's family. We want to promise again what our godparents promised for us—that we will live in Jesus' love. Because we are members of God's family, Jesus will give us a special sign of his life and love today. He will be present with us through his Body and Blood. We begin to share our joy at his coming by our song.

Entrance song: "Here We Are" (Repp, FEL). As the entrance song begins the child walks up the center aisle accompanied by his parents and the celebrant. The child carries a decorated, unlit candle, which he places near the lighted Easter candle in the sanctuary. He stands there to renew his baptismal promises.

Opening prayer (*by the priest*): Our Father, we are here in the name of your Son and at his invitation. You made this day to bring joy to (*child's name or names of several children*) and his family. (*Child's name*), when you were baptized you were not old enough to promise God that you would be his loving child. Today you will be able to tell God what your godparents said for you. The first time you received a gift of special love from God the Father, was on the day of your baptism. You were called to be a child of God. Now that you are growing to love God more, make your own promise to him.

Child (*standing before the Easter candle with outstretched arms in a gesture of reverence*): God, my Father, today before you, my family and friends I want to make my own baptismal promises. Jesus, I want to live more like you and grow as a loving and forgiving child. At holy communion you will give me your life and strength to live my baptism. I will get this help from the Father, the Son and the Holy Spirit.

Child turns to the community and says: Mom and Dad, I thank you for the gift of baptism and for your example to help me live like Jesus.

Child turns to candle, puts his hand on the Easter candle and says loud enough for all to hear: Jesus, you can do all things. I know you love me so I want to say together with everyone here the prayer you taught us, the Our Father. (Here everyone says the Lord's Prayer together.)

Priest: Jesus taught us how to pray and in today's Epistle of St. Paul, he reminds us how to live. (The following adaptation is written in script on stationary and read to the child by his father, another member of the family or parish. After the reading the script is placed in an envelope and presented to the child.)

Reading I: Adapted from Phil. 1:1-6.

Ephesus, in Turkey, January 18, 54 A.D.

From Paul and from the persons who are with us, to our parents and all other friends of Jesus who meet in your house; wishing you the grace and peace of God our Father and the Lord Jesus. (*If there is only one first communicant, mention the parents, brothers and sisters by name.*)

I always mention you in my prayers and thank God for you, because I hear of the love and the faith which you have for the Lord Jesus and all the saints. I pray that this faith will rise to a sense of fellowship that will show you all the good things that we are able to do for Christ. My prayer is that your love for each other may increase more and more and that your knowledge may deepen so that you can always recognize and do what is good and right.

You are about to be admitted for the first time in your life to the breaking of the bread. This is what I received from the Lord, and in turn pass on to you: on the same night on which he was betrayed, the Lord Jesus took some bread, and thanked God for it and broke it. Giving it to his friends he said, "This is my Body, which is for you: do this as a memorial of me." In the same way he took the cup after supper and said, "This cup is the new covenant of my Blood. Whenever you drink it, do this as a memorial of me." The fact that there is only one loaf means that, although there are many of us, we form a single body because we all have a share in this one loaf.

Thus, pray for all people. Greet all with the holy kiss. My orders, in the Lord's name, are that this letter is to be read to all the brothers and sisters. The grace of our Lord Jesus be with you.

Response by all present: Surely, if we listen to God's word with love and joy, it will grow in our minds and hearts. Let us try to understand the power of the word of God by living as members of God's family. This is the way others will know that we are his friends. *(Note: the response may also be in the form of a song.)*

Reading II: John 6:35-41.

Homily: After the priest has read the gospel he invites the first communicant to come up and has a conversation (dialogue homily) with the child about the Gospel and the significance of the day.

Jesus tells us that we must love God as trustingly as a child loves his parents. In St. Matthew's story we can understand what Jesus is telling us. One day Jesus called a child to him and, putting him among the disciples, he said to them, "Unless you become like children, you will never enter into the Kingdom of Heaven. Whoever becomes like this child is the greatest in the kingdom of heaven. If anyone shows real concern for a child like this in my name, he is showing his love for me" *(adapted from Matt. 19:14).*

Prayer of the faithful: Father, you are interested and concerned about all our needs. We ask you to grant the things we need at this moment. *(Priest pauses and asks the first communicants and/or family and friends to add their intentions.)* Father, you know what is best for each of us. With your understanding of our needs may these requests be given to each of us.

Offertory:

Song: "Take Our Bread" (Joe Wise, FEL). The child carries the ciborium; the parents carry the water and wine, pour them into the chalice and return to their places.

Prayer over gifts: God our Father, we come before you with gifts of bread and wine to show that we are yours. These gifts say that you have given us your Son, Jesus. We want to share this bread and wine as your people—giving ourselves to Jesus through everyone present here today.

Priest: Pray, friends that our gift and this sacrifice will be accepted by God our Father.
People: Lord, please accept this sacrifice to show our praise and thanks for the good we have received as your family.
Priest: The Lord is with each of you.
People: And also with you.
Priest: Lift up your hearts.
People: We lift them up to the Lord.
Priest: Let us give thanks to God our Father.
People: It is good to give him thanks.

Eucharistic prayer:

Preface: For coming to live among us, we thank you Lord Jesus.
For teaching us about God our Father, . . .
For rising from the dead and giving us new life, . . .
For coming to us in Holy Communion, . . .
For sending your spirit to live with us today and always, . . .

Adaptation of canon: Father, you are very good; you give us the gift of life and all that we have—our parents, our friends, and all who have helped us to love Jesus more.

Father, look at our gifts of bread and wine. Send your Holy Spirit to bless these gifts. Make them the Body and Blood of your Son, Jesus Christ. On the night before he died for us he held bread in his hands. He thanked his Father. Then breaking the bread he gave it to his friends and said, "Eat this. It is my Body which I will give up for you." After supper, he took the cup of wine in his hands. Again he gave you thanks. He gave the cup to his friends and said, "All of you drink from this cup. Here is my Blood, the gift that was promised to you because you are my friends. I will shed my blood willingly to free all people from sin. Do this as I have shown you. This meal is to be a remembrance of all the good things I have done for you in the past, and a sign that I will always be with you." We believe that Christ has died, Christ is risen, Christ will come again. Father, we no longer offer bread and wine to you. We offer you Jesus, your Son and our brother. With Jesus we want to offer ourselves to you.

Bless us, Father with your Spirit of love. As we share in this supper, teach us to live as your children. We want to offer our prayers and our lives with all the people in heaven and on earth through Jesus, your Son. All glory and honor is yours through Christ, in the unity of the Holy Spirit forever and ever. Amen.

(The priest invites the child by name to receive communion with his or her parents. The adults may receive under both species if they wish, but this may be omitted because children usually do not like the taste of wine.)

Communion song: "Love One Another" (Sister Germaine, FEL); "Bread He Has Given Us" (Joe Wise, FEL); "Look Beyond" (Ducote, FEL).

Prayer after communion: Jesus, you make us happy by coming to us in so many ways. Thank you for being with us today in the form of bread and wine shared with our family and friends. Help us to know and love you more each time you come to us in holy communion.

Before the blessing the child takes his unlit candle and lights it from the Paschal candle as a symbol of the new presence of Jesus. He then stands in front of the celebrant as the priest gives the final blessing.

Final blessing: May almighty God bless you (*child's name*) and all here present in the name of the Father and of the Son and of the Holy Spirit.

Dismissal: Let us go now and continue to celebrate the joy of the Lord's coming with our family and friends!

People: Thank you, Jesus.

The child, his parents and the priest lead the people out of the place of worship.

Closing song:

- "Allelu" (Ray Repp, FEL).
- "Let All the Earth" (Dameans, FEL).
- "They'll Know" (Scholtes, FEL).

Follow-up: Celebrate the occasion with a special meal together.

SAMPLE LITURGIES
SUITABLE FOR INTERMEDIATE GRADES

Life Themes:
- Creation: Light
- Relationships: Friendship
- Festivals: Scout Sunday

Liturgical Themes:
- Church Year: All Saints
- Sacraments: First Penance

CREATION: LIGHT

Theme: As the child begins to develop abstract thinking ability we can introduce themes such as the light-darkness contrast in scripture. This celebration makes use of the child's fascination with light, acknowledges its value and points to scriptural symbolism.

Materials and preparation:
- Lower intermediate grades would especially enjoy making candles personally, either by dipping process or by molding them in half-pint milk cartons.
- The local synagogue or library might supply personnel or materials for an understanding of the Jewish feast of lights (Channukah). This would be more meaningful for the upper intermediate grades.
- The most ideal setting would be at night, in a darkened area or under a star-filled sky. Another setting might include candles of all sizes, shapes, and colors. Torches or tiki-lamps could be used.
- The celebration centers around the Paschal candle. Talented fifth and sixth graders could take charge of decorating the candle for Easter. (Use tempera paint mixed on a bar of Ivory soap. It will adhere to the wax well this way.)

Celebration introduction: Close your eyes for a minute. Imagine that you were blind or that the whole world was without light. How difficult it would be to move, or enjoy colors, or recognize a friend or even some danger. Light is one of the most important things we have although we often take it for granted. Jesus compared himself and his message to light. He said, "I am the light of the world." He was saying that he was important to us. Today we celebrate how important he is.

Entrance song: "Sounds of Silence" (Simon and Garfunkel) playing in the background. Have darkness as the celebrant sits amidst the group in silence. Then he lights the Paschal candle or another large candle.

Greeting: May the light of Christ be with you to guide your path.
Response: And also with you.

Penitential rite: We can choose darkness instead of light. We can turn off the switch, blow out the candle. Worse than that, we can live as people of darkness, choosing sin instead of goodness. Let's stop and think of the times, the ways, the people we have left in the darkness by not choosing Christ the Light, his way and his love. *(Pause.)*

Lord, have mercy.
Christ, have mercy.
Lord, have mercy.

Gloria: Glory to God and peace to his people. God our Father, we worship you; we give you thanks. We praise you for sending Jesus our brother as the Light of the world. Jesus, only son of God, we ask you to take away the darkness of sin and hear our prayer. Help us to accept the Spirit, who offers love and grace to us. Glory be to the Father, Son and Spirit forever and ever. Amen.

Opening prayer: Ask a student to compose a special prayer for the occasion.

Reading I: Rosemary Haughton, *Listen to Love* (Winona, Minn.: St. Mary's Press), p. 256.

Response: Psalm 23 (Be a light for my path, O Lord).

Reading II:
- Exodus 13:17-22.
- Luke 11:1-9.
- John 1:1-12.

Homily: Discuss the importance of light and Jesus as our way in darkness. Include the ideas of seeing our daily life in "a new light" and becoming children of light as fourth, fifth, and sixth graders.

Prayer of the faithful: Just as light penetrates the darkness we know that our prayers move out to a loving Father, aware of our needs. So we bring them before him today.

Response: Be a light to us, O Lord.

For a church with its Pope, bishops and people who want to know
 God's love and experience his presence, we pray . . .
For our country and our world that its leaders may in wisdom guide

men toward peace, we pray . . .

For each student in our school that he might learn to follow Jesus as a guide and be a light to one another, we pray . . .

That God may shed light on specific problems we face locally, especially _____, we pray . . .

Priest: We have spoken to you from the darkness of our life and problems and trust that you will be with us, O Lord. Strengthen us and help us to live as children of light through Jesus, Light of the world. Amen.

Offertory song: With our gifts of bread and wine we also offer our lives. We welcome Jesus into our lives and promise to let him shine through us. We join in our offering song: "This Little Light of Mine" (traditional).

Prayer over gifts: Father, just as light is so necessary to life, so too bread and wine are important food and drink. Through your Spirit may they become Jesus' own body and blood and strengthen and enlighten our lives.

Eucharistic rite: God we are happy that you are our loving Father. We thank you for giving us your very own Son as a man. He is our light, teaching us how to live. When we listen to Jesus we learn what you, our Father, are like. And so with all people living now and those who have lived before us; with all who will follow us and, most of all, with those here together right now we say with all our heart: Holy, holy, holy, Lord God of hosts, Heaven and Earth are filled with your glory. Hosanna in the highest. Blessed is he who comes in the name of the Lord. Hosanna in the highest.

Canon: Use canon 2 or 3.

Communion rite:

Song: Just as we look beyond the light to its source in a candle or light bulb or the sun, we look beyond the sign of bread and wine to Jesus, the Light of the world, as we sing: "Look Beyond" (Ducote, FEL).

Response: Let us remember that when we were presented with a candle at our baptism we promised to be the Light of Jesus to the world. We now light our candles from the Paschal candle and promise to love God and each other.

Do you promise to avoid sin and darkness in your life?

I promise.
Do you promise to learn about Jesus our Light so you might follow his example?
I promise.
Do you promise to shine with love for each other?
I promise.
Father, you have heard our promises. Help us to walk in Jesus' light and be signs of his love for all men. Amen.

Dismissal: Go in peace to be a sign of Jesus' light and love.

Response: Thanks be to God.

Closing song: Jesus has filled us with his light and love; he has shared his Body and Blood. As we close our liturgy we join our voices to sing "Sing Out His Goodness" (Ducote, FEL).

Follow-up:

- With the children visit a synagogue and meet with the rabbi.
- Prepare a Channukah ceremony leaflet for the child to take home and celebrate.
- Celebrate with a "searchlight" game to find hidden prizes with flashlights.
- Invite an amateur astronomer to speak with the children and demonstrate with pictures or equipment. Or visit a planetarium or observatory.

FRIENDSHIP: YOU'VE GOT A FRIEND

Theme: Friendship is something that gives richness to our lives as we begin to mature. The intermediate grade student gathers a circle of friends—usually in the Scout Troop or the neighborhood ball team. We celebrate Jesus as a special friend too.

Materials and preparation:

- A brief series of dramas prepared by the children illustrating negative and positive aspects of friendship could be used as a theme setter or homily.

- Write a letter to a friend who lives far away; present it at the offertory and mail afterward. A friend who is not part of the usual community could be invited to the liturgy and the celebration afterward.
- Bring a dessert to be shared in friendship at a party after the liturgy.
- Participants should make a promise to help someone with a project, befriend a lonely person, or help their parents or an older neighbor.
- Flags of many nations may be used as decor to bring out the broadest areas of friendship.
- The movie "Neighbors" (National Film Board of Canada, Mackenzie Bldg., 1 Lombard St., Toronto) is a good illustration of the lack of friendship.
- Make a series of "Friendship is . . ." posters for the procession.

Celebration introduction: We are to be friends with one another in the same way that Jesus is our friend. We want to love each other as Jesus loves us. (*Procession with posters on which are illustrations by each class or student*, "Friendship is . . .")

Entrance song:

- "Hand in Hand" (Wise, World Library of Sacred Music) or

● "Give Me Your Hand" (Blue, FEL)

Penitential rite: God our Father extended a sign of love when he sent Jesus to be our brother. But we don't always accept Jesus or one another. Let's acknowledge our sins, especially our lack of friendship as we pray.

I confess to God, to all the saints and to you my friends, that I have failed to love God and you my brothers and sisters in what I said and did, and in what I failed to do. I ask God, the saints and each of you to forgive me and help me to live in friendship and love. Amen.

Opening prayer: Father, we are together today to learn how to remember you and one another in all we do. Help us to give ourselves to you and to each other. We ask this in Jesus' name. Amen.

Reading I: *A Friend Is Someone Who Likes You* by Joan Walsh Anglund (Harcourt, Brace & World, Inc., 1958).

Response: Listen and meditate on "You've Got A Friend" by Carole King (Columbia Music Company).

Reading II: John 15:12-17.

Homily: Allow the children to develop a dialog homily on the value of friendship or use drama as described in the first suggestion of "Materials and Preparation."

Offertory song: We all fail in friendship at times but we want to be brothers and sisters in Jesus. We bring our lives, our offerings, our problems with Jesus to the Father as we sing "Come In Pilgrim" (Ault, FEL).

Prayer over gifts: Father, accept our struggles and efforts to be friends of each other and of Jesus our brother. Join them to our gifts of bread and wine and strengthen our friendships. We ask this through your Spirit, God forever and ever. Amen.

Eucharistic rite: Use the canon on friendship from James Dallens' *Liturgical Celebrations: Possible Patterns*, National American Liturgy Resources, Cincinnati, Ohio, 1971, p. 40 ff. If unavailable, another canon may be substituted.

Communion rite: Each of us needs the support of one another in a friendship with Jesus or with each other. This is the theme of our meditation song at communion.

Song: "Bridge Over Troubled Water" (Simon and Garfunkel, Columbia Records).

Response: Friendship remains just an idea unless we make it real. Let's pause to greet each other as friends. (*An alternative response might be:* let's make a promise to help a neighbor in need. OR *pass around a scroll which reads:* "We promise to be friends to each other." Each person signs the scroll as he receives it.)

Prayer: Father, thank you for Jesus our friend whose Body and Blood we have received in communion. Help us to strengthen our friendship with the help of your Spirit. We ask this in Jesus' name. Amen.

Dismissal: Let us go forth in friendship to love and serve the Lord.

Response: Thanks be to God.

Our closing song reminds us that to be friends of one another and of Jesus here in church is not enough. We have to be friends always, so we sing: "Turn Your Eyes" (Ducote, FEL).

Follow-up: Mail the letters. Report back to the group on success in carrying out the pledges of service. Share the dessert and celebrate friendship.

SCOUT SUNDAY:
DOING MY DUTY TO GOD AND MY COUNTRY

Theme: Youth in the intermediate grades are great "joiners." Parents are proud to see and celebrate their children's achievements. This liturgy originally celebrated at a Sunday parish liturgy, celebrates the value of such groups and their contributions to the community of God's people.

Materials and preparation:
- Most of the symbols will be drawn from the ceremonies and insignia of the group itself (in this case, Girl Scouts). Materials should be prepared in advance and some brief practice held so that the entire celebration is clear in the minds of those participating.
- Handout materials or bulletin inserts can be used to instruct those present about the Scouts.
- Make a blank American flag from a 3'x5' piece of plywood. Cover it in red felt and attach a blue star field. The flag should be placed on an easel in front of the altar. A blue felt cross should be made to be attached later to the top of the flag.
- Scouts in uniform act as ushers, servers, readers at the celebration.

Celebration introduction: Welcome to the mass celebrating National Girl Scout Sunday. On behalf of the Girl Scouts throughout the United States and the world, we greet you. Each Scout makes a promise as a part of her scouting activities. It begins: "On my honor I will try to do my duty to God and my country . . ." We have chosen as the theme for today's mass "Doing my duty to God and my country."

Entrance song: Presentation of the American flag followed by the priest. All sing "Star Spangled Banner."

Penitential rite: God our Father, we gather here in the name of your Son and at his invitation. Jesus, you call us friend and brother. You gave us one commandment—that our love for each other be real. Only then will others know that we are your friends. Give us your help to be strong that we may know ourselves and our faults. Let us call to mind the sins we may have committed this past week (*pause*). May almighty God have mercy on us, forgive us our sins, and bring us to everlasting life.

Response: Amen.

Reading I: Preamble to the Constitution of the Girl Scouts of America found in the *Leader's Notebook*.

Reading II (*Speaker 1*): There are six fundamentals that a Girl Scout strives for in her years of scouting. Each one helps us to do our duty to God and country as well as help other people. We would like to explain those six fundamentals for you today. We have chosen a blank American flag to help us. The flag is a symbol of the United States of America, our country. Each of the patrols in our troop will place one white stripe on the flag and explain the fundamental it represents.

Speaker 2 (service): One of the songs we sing says, "We are made for service to care for all men . . ." Life can be so empty when nobody cares; life can be so empty when nobody shares. But if man gives himself to help other men, the happiness of Christ will live within us. A Scout is dedicated to service in the home, in the school, in the church, and in the community. Helping with the chores at home and taking care of younger brothers and sisters, participating in ecology projects, community drives and school clean-up campaigns, planting trees, feeding needy families and service projects to old folks' homes are all ways in which a Girl Scout is of service. *(Speaker places white stripe on flag for service.)*

Speaker 3 (democratic form of government): A Girl Scout learns what a vote means by having a chance to select and plan activities. This is a good foundation for our future. Sometimes we have to go by the will of the majority even if it wasn't our choice, but that too, is part of democratic government. We have our own executive council meetings called Court of Honor and decide on our own schedule of activities. Thus we are learning to be democratic in the way we think, vote, and act. *(Speaker 3 places white stripe on the flag for democracy.)*

Speaker 4 (citizenship): Scouting teaches us that doing our duty to our country means being a good citizen right now. Citizenship starts in our own home and Scout troop. It means doing what we have promised to do, when we are supposed to do it. It means being at the right place on time. It means caring about the success of our troop, our school, our church, and our home. The duties of citizenship are many and in Scouting we are trying to practice them. *(Speaker 4 places white stripe for citizenship.)*

Speaker 5 (health and safety): Safety rules are a part of any Girl

Scout activity. Learning to care for ourselves, and to help others is part of doing our duty to God and our fellow countrymen. We learn first aid and home nursing. While working on various badges, we learn the things necessary to make our homes and lives safe and healthy. (*Speaker 5 places white stripes for health and safety.*)

Speaker 6 (*international friendship*): We belong to an association of Girl Scouts and Girl Guides throughout the world. We wear the World Association Pin on our uniforms to show that we are members of an international organization. Planning the programs for special Scout celebrations throughout the year helps us to learn more about our friends and neighbors and to remember that God said, "Whatsoever you do to the least of my brethren, that you do unto me." (*Speaker 6 places white stripe on flag.*)

Speaker I: A Girl Scout makes a threefold promise which begins with duty to God and country. The second part is a pledge to help other people at all times and the third is to obey the Girl Scout laws. The laws are a simple means of expressing all of these six fundamentals of scouting.

The fifty stars, each representing a state in our United States and symbolizing that we are a part of four million scouts throughout the U.S., will be placed on the blue field by the Brownie Troops. (*Fifty stars placed on the blue field. Dots should be placed ahead of time to indicate placement of stars.*)

The flag is a symbol of our country and the cross a symbol of our love of God and our willingness to do our duty as Christians. We place this cross atop the flag uniting the two and forming a symbol of a Girl Scout's duty to God and country.

Reading III: We now listen to a story from Jesus about that duty. Mark 2:23-3:6.

Homily:

- Man lives as a Christian within society.
- God works through man in society.
- God's work must truly be our own daily activities.

Prayer of the faithful: The prayer is begun by speaker 1 and each troup represented offers an intention.

Response: We pray to the Lord.

For Girl Scouts throughout the world . . .
That all Scouts may be good citizens of their home, school, troop, church, and community . . .

Other intentions.

Offertory (*Speaker 2*): At this time we present the Girl Scout Flag as a symbol of Girl Scouting and place it near the altar to unite scouting with God. The flag is followed by trefoils from each of the troops represented here today. The trefoil is the emblem of Girl Scouting representing each of the three parts of the Girl Scout promise. *(Trefoils with troop numbers are carried forward and taped to the front of the altar.)*

Offertory song: "Lord Accept the Gifts We Offer"
The gifts are brought forward by the leaders of the different troops represented. Each gives much time and energy to help young girls learn about their duty to God and country. The candles each is carrying symbolize a willingness to serve and "to light one little candle," to do good rather than curse the darkness.

Prayer over gifts: Father, accept our gifts of bread and wine along with all of our acts of service in the past and our pledge of service in the future. Strengthen us through this eucharist and enlighten us through your Spirit that we may be good and faithful citizens. This we ask of you, Father, forever and ever. Amen.

Eucharistic rite: Use regular Sunday preface and canon.

Communion hymn: "Whatsoever You Do" (Jabusch, FEL).

Prayer: Father, thank you for our country. Thank you for our Scouts. Thank you for our Church. Thank you especially for this eucharist. Amen.

Dismissal: Priest gives blessing.

Speaker 1: Would you please stand for the retiring of the colors. Procession with American and Girl Scout flags.

Closing song: All of us need to join our Scouts in love of each other and service to our community. Our closing song is a reminder. "They'll Know We Are Christians" (Scholtas, FEL).

Follow-up: The troops should engage in specific service projects such as helping a shut-in, cleaning around the church, or helping with a parish baby-sitting service.

ALL THE SAINTS: SINNERS WHO KEPT TRYING

Theme: Great fun is in store for the trick or treaters but there is also a need to give reflection and celebration on the "Hallows" of Halloween. This liturgy portrays saints as real people and offers hope that we can follow in their footsteps.

Materials and preparation:
- Costuming and one or two brief skits could be one way of enriching the celebration. A group of children might be dressed as the twelve apostles and Mary.
- Banners of one's patron saint or a special class patron could be prepared to adorn the sanctuary.
- Essays and portrayals of "contemporary saints" should be encouraged, e.g., Vietnamese casualties, flood and earthquake victims.
- A mobile with pictures or quotations from saints throughout history could be placed as a focal point over the altar.

Celebration introduction: We have many people who are heroes to us such as the astronauts or a football figure. The saints are our heroes too, not because they always made touchdowns but because they kept on trying and finally scored by their whole lives. Let's sing in their honor "When the Saints Go Marching In" (traditional).

Penitential rite: As we prepare to celebrate our calling to love Jesus as the saints did, we call to mind the way in which we have not answered the call.
You have called us to be saints of God . . . Lord, have mercy.
You have shown us the way by our saintly heroes . . . Christ have mercy.
You pardon us for not answering your call . . . Lord, have mercy.

Gloria: Sing "Glory to God" (Repp, World Library of Sacred Music).

Opening prayer: Father you are with us showing us your love in all creation. Christ our brother has shown us how to be saints. Help us to remember his example and live in your love. We ask this through the Holy Spirit. Amen.

Reading I: Have several of the students give a brief sketch of what their patron saint did and what he or she means to them.

Reading II: Revelation 7:2-4 and 9-14.

Reading III: Matthew 25:31-46 (should be adapted).

Homily: Saints are not extraordinary people so much as people who did the ordinary things extraordinarily well. That's what it means "to be in that number when the saints go marching in."

Creed: We believe in God, Father of all men. He has called us to work together to build a new world of unity and peace. We believe in Jesus Christ, Son of God, our Savior and Lord who suffered and died and rose again for us. He did this that we might learn to live for others and find hope in his victory over death. We believe in the Spirit, in the power of truth, peace, and love. We believe in the Church, the unity and fellowship to which all men are called. We pray that we may heal this broken world and find a new and better life through Christ our brother. Amen.

Offertory song:

- "All That We Have" (Ault, FEL), or
- "Service" (Caesar, FEL).

Prayer over gifts: Father, our simple gifts of bread and wine remind us of the many simple ways which your saints found to serve you. Help us to imitate them as we share these gifts in the name of your Son and the Spirit. Amen.

Eucharistic rite (Preface): We thank you, good Father, for giving us this day to live together for you. You have invited us to be your saints by living today fully as human beings. You even sent Christ to live as man and to show us the way. You are patient despite our stumbling and falling. You are always present to help us to begin again. We praise you with all creation as we sing "Holy, Holy, Holy . . ." ("Missa Bossa Nova")

Father, you have indeed shown your love in the coming of Jesus, our brother and light of the world. We want to walk in his light and enlighten others by our lives. We offer our lives and these gifts as we recall that the day before he suffered he took bread into his hands and looking up to you Father, he said thanks, broke the bread and gave it to his disciples, saying, "Take and eat for this is my Body." After this he took the cup and said thanks, blessed it and handed it to his disciples, saying, "Take and drink this all of you, for this is the cup of my Blood, the cup of the new and everlasting covenant. Do this in memory of me."

Response: Now that we eat this bread and drink this cup, we proclaim Jesus' death and resurrection.

Celebrant: We ask you Father, to accept these gifts. Fill us with your Spirit who strengthens all your saints that we may renew the earth today and come to be united with Christ our brother. Through him, and with him and in him you receive Father, with the Spirit all honor and glory forever. Amen.

Communion song:

- "Song of St. Francis" (Teleketics Productions) or
- "Sing Out His Goodness" (Ducote, FEL)

Response: Let us pause to remember and give thanks for our patron saint whose name we bear _____. Let us be thankful for Mary, the patroness of our United States and _____ the patron of our parish. Let us be thankful for our dead relatives and friends who gave good example to us. Let us remember other saints of today who shared the good news (Martin Luther King, Dorothy Day, Mother Theresa, Thomas Merton, John Kennedy, Dag Hammarskjold).

Father, thank you for all those who led us to you by their example, especially our brother Jesus. Keep us strong with your love so we may serve all men. Amen.

Dismissal: Let us go forth as saints to love and serve God and each other.

Response: Thanks be to God.

Closing Song:

- "Witness Song" (Ault, FEL) or
- "New Creation" (Ault, FEL) or
- "Glory Land" (Ault, FEL).

Follow-up: Share the skits with another class or other parish members.

PENANCE: "A NEW PROMISE"

Theme: Growing friendship brings the sharing of secrets and the making or promises. To sin is to betray our promise of love to God and each other. Reconciliation can be seen as a renewal of the promise to be a special person of love.

Materials and preparation:
- Small cutouts of oneself on which has been noted a resolution of change can be prepared ahead of time. During the entrance procession these can be individually taped onto a large, house-shaped poster representing the family of God.
- A filmstrip on the prodigal son and loving father can be used.
- Dramatization of two or three life situations with their resolutions can be arranged.

Celebration introduction: *The students may assemble in advance with a number of priests gathered to hear their confession. Absolution may be given during the penitential rite. After the confessions we begin* . . . God our loving Father calls us to come to him for forgiveness. As we assemble we recall his invitation and we sing.

Entrance song: "Come In Pilgrim" (Ault, FEL).

Greeting: God our Father is willing to forgive us if we are willing to forgive each other. As a "penance" for those going to confession; as a sign of thanks for God's forgiveness let us speak to each other some words of greeting and peace. *(Pause for "peace sign.")*

Penitential rite: Father, keep us always in your peace. Help us through your son Jesus to see you more clearly, follow you, and love you more dearly. In the Spirit we ask this. Amen.

Reading I: Select a few clippings from the daily newspaper that illustrate a failure to love. Read and summarize them. Another option is to have the children write stories of their own or another's failure to love.

Response: Read one of the penitential psalms.

Reading II:
- The forgiving father—Luke 15:11-24 or
- The Last Judgment—Matthew 25:31-41 or
- The Parable of the Talents—Matthew 25:14-30.

Homily:
- God calls us to be the best person we can be.
- We waste our talents, find excuses, fail to share.
- God keeps calling and forgiving if we are willing to try again.

Prayer of the faithful: Have the students write the petitions and use the sung response "Hear, O Lord" (Repp, FEL).

Offertory song: Have a special group prepare an offertory song or use the Teleketics record "Sounds of Love."

Prayer over gifts: Father, here is bread made from grains of wheat that are crushed as we are sometimes crushed by sin. Here is wine made from many grapes which were produced by the love we would like to have. Yet these two gifts and our own efforts will be made special through your love. Accept these gifts which will become the Body and Blood of your son given for us. Amen.

Eucharistic rite: Use canon II.

Communion song: Play "I Am a Rock" from *Sounds of Silence* (Simon and Garfunkel, Columbia Records).

Read from "Devotions Upon Emergent Occasions," Meditation XVII by John Donne ". . . No man is an island" accompanied by the flute or guitar background.

Response: We all need one another to survive, to grow. Let us think about some kind word or deed we want to share with someone after mass.

Prayer: Father, thank you for calling us back to you and feeding us with the banquet of Jesus your Son. We want to be your servants in love, so strengthen us by your Spirit. Amen.

Dismissal: Sin is saying "no" to God. We are now resolved to live a new life. We sing out that resolution.

Closing song: "Gonna Give You A Yes, Lord" (Ducote, FEL).

Follow-up:

- Remind the students of their post-communion resolutions.
- Have a carefully controlled "bonfire" to burn clippings of "bad news—sin" used in the liturgy.
- Develop a "healing experience" through a class project.

SAMPLE LITURGIES
SUITABLE FOR JUNIOR HIGH SCHOOL

Life Themes:
- Creation: Life
- Relationships: Loneliness
- Festivals: End of the School Year

Liturgical Themes:
- Church Year: Advent
- Sacraments: Confirmation

LIFE—TO BE ALIVE!

Theme: Nowhere is the *joie de vivre* so evident and nowhere is the pain of growing so keen as in the adolescent years. This liturgy is a reflection on that joy and a prayer for the painfulness.

Materials and preparation:

- A large banner proclaiming "The Glory of God Is Man Fully Alive" (St. Irenaeus) or a large poster of Snoopy dancing ("Peanuts") should be prepared.
- Visuals of the story of Lazarus might be used, perhaps with slides contrasting with pictures of graves. ("Good News" filmstrip, ROA films, 1696 N. Astor St., Milwaukee, Wisc. 53202.)
- A scrapbook of "My Life" or pictures of life and death could be used at offertory time. Daily newspaper clippings offer good resources.
- A poem composed by students about personal reflections on life might be used as a theme setter or communion meditation. A good example is E. E. Cummings' poem "I thank you God for this most amazing Day."
- Ideas concerning the challenge of life, understanding senior citizens, the abortion question are all appropriate to ninth grade students. A segment of the 16mm movie "Night and Fog" could be used to set a tone of death. ("Night and Fog," Argus Films, available at McGraw-Hill, Inc., 330 W. 42nd St., New York, N.Y. 10036.)

Celebration introduction: God has created us and given us life but so often we really fail to live as he would have us live. We get carried along amid hectic activities and never take time to reflect upon life and what it is all about. For a few moments we would like to pause and think about life and how we can live it more fully.

Entrance song: "To be Alive" (Repp, FEL).

Opening prayer: O God we praise you for your gift of life. We bless you for coming to live with us in a special way at baptism. Help us to live truly pleasing lives. We ask this through Jesus our brother who lives with you and the Spirit forever. Amen.

Penitential rite:

Priest: In the name of the Father, and of the Son, and of the Holy Spirit.
All: Amen.
Priest: May the grace of our Lord Jesus Christ and the love of God and the fellowship of the Holy Spirit be with all of you.
All: And also with you.
Priest: Let us acknowledge our sins so that we may be fit to celebrate the sacred mysteries.

Commentator: Lord, we are sorry for the wrong we have done.
All: Lord, Have mercy.
Commentator: At times we try to do what is right, and sometimes we don't care to try.
All: Christ have mercy.
Commentator: Help us in the battles of our life. Even if they are small battles, they are still important to our lives.
All: Lord, have mercy.

Priest: Glory to God in heaven.
All: And peace to his people on earth . . .

Prayer by priest: This prayer should reflect the present life situation of the group with a plea to the Father to help us maintain our balance in life especially through the eucharist.

Reading I: Selection from *The Diary of Anne Frank*.

Response: Silent meditation.

Reading II: Genesis 37 (shortened and adapted if necessary) or students might dramatize this.
Response: "All of My Life" (Sr. Germaine, FEL).

Reading III: John 11:25-26 ("I am the resurrection . . .") Or use filmstrip of the story of Lazarus, Good News Film, #18.

Homily:
- The strongest desire is to live—we must respect life.
- Jesus is the life giver.

● Our response to Jesus should be the fully human quality of our lives.

Prayer of the faithful:

Response: We thank you, Lord.

For the gift of God's life given to us at baptism . . .
For being alive and able to praise you . . .
For our parents and friends who share their lives with us . . .
For being able to smell the beautiful flowers and feel the warmth of your sun . . .
For all the birds and butterflies and all your living creatures which add so much beauty to the world and give us pleasure . . .
For leaders who understand the beauty of life and have the courage to foster life . . .

Offertory: Scrapbooks, pictures, clippings (described above) could be brought to the altar and the students gather around it and sing.

Offertory song: "All Our Joy" (Ducote, FEL).

Prayer over gifts: Accept Father, ourselves, our friends and all the wonders of life which we offer you through this sign of bread and wine.

Blessed are you, O Lord, God of all creation. Through your goodness we have this bread to offer, which earth has given and human hands have made. It will become for us the bread of life.
All: Blessed be God forever.
Blessed are you, Lord, God of all creation. Through your goodness we have this wine, the fruit of the vine and work of human hands. It will become our spiritual drink.
All: Blessed be God forever.

Priest: Pray, brethren that our sacrifice may be acceptable to God, the almighty Father.
All: May the Lord accept the sacrifice at your hands for the praise and glory of his name, for our good and the good of all his Church.

Eucharistic prayer: God, we are happy that you are our all-powerful and loving Father. And we thank you for giving us your very own Son as a man. He teaches us how to live when we have faith in him. When we look at Jesus, we can see what you are like, Father.

And so, with all your other creatures here, with the elements of nature, with all people who are living and with those who have lived before us; with babies who are born today and those that will be born tomorrow, with all people who will ever live and most of all with all who are here together now, we say:

Holy, Holy, Holy Lord, God our Father, maker of us and of all things. Everything is full of your goodness and love. We are grateful to you forever for your son Jesus Christ, Alleluia.

Eucharistic rite: Use canon III.

Communion song: Play "Peace Prayer of St. Francis" (Teleketics, Los Angeles, Cal.)

Response: After a bit of silence, sing the "Peace Prayer" as a collection is taken up for a "life" charity.

Prayer: Father, we thank you for Jesus who is our way, truth, and light. Keep us strong in him that we may show forth your good news to all men. We ask this through your Spirit. Amen.

Dismissal: Life is not possible unless it is given. Our parents shared its physical aspects with us. Jesus and his people, the Church, shared a deeper life of grace. Let us go forth to proclaim both dimensions in the name of the Father and of the Son and of the Spirit. Amen.

Closing song: "You Fill the Day" (Wise, World Library of Sacred Music).

Follow-up:
- Send the collection donation to "Another Mother for Peace," CARE, "Campaign for Human Development" or another life charity.
- Engage in an ecology project which would show the happy cooperation of the class and foster a better quality of life (e.g., clean up a local stream).

LONELINESS: LEAVE ME ALONE!

Theme: There is a time to be silent and a time to speak. There is a time that we need to be alone but also times when we are lonely. The teen struggles with this feeling and faces the struggle in this liturgy.

Materials and preparation:
- As the students are seated for the liturgy of the word the chairs may be arranged in a large circle facing *outward*, so that no one has eye contact with another. After the penance service and peace greeting the chairs are turned inward for the remainder of the celebration. As an alternative the room could be in darkness with the song "You've Got A Friend" (Carole King) playing in the background. After the penance service, partially light the room, especially the lectern. At the offertory turn on all the lights.
- The film "String Bean" (Contemporary McGraw Hill, 330 W. 42nd St., New York, N.Y. 10036) shows loneliness and the redeeming love of an old lady. It would fit into this theme quite well.
- Write and share reflections of Jesus' thoughts while he was alone in the desert before his public life began or as he saw his apostles asleep in the garden on Holy Thursday evening.
- Prepare gifts to be presented at the offertory; later to be shared with a lonely shut-in.

Celebration introduction: Today's music is filled with the theme of man's loneliness. If we think about it we know how much everyone needs a friend. Let's think of all the lonely people and pray for their needs.

Entrance song: Play a recording of "Eleanor Rigby" (Beatles) or "Richard Cory" and provide words in a dittoed program.

Penitential rite: God, you are our loving Father who gives food and song to men's lives so we pray, Lord have mercy. Jesus, you came to give light and joy to those in darkness and sadness so we pray, Christ have mercy. Spirit of God, you bring love and warmth to this lonely and cold earth so we pray, Lord have mercy.

Opening prayer: Father, we recall how often it is said that no man is an island. As you sent Jesus to be our brother, send him today in this mass to fill us with your Spirit of love. Amen.

Reading I: Silent meditation on loneliness.

Reading II: Selections from David's Psalms.
Response: Sing "Pause Awhile" (Ault FEL).

Reading III: Matthew 26:36-46 (Jesus in the garden).

Homily: Some have fun together and some are turned away, but too many are simply ignored, forgotten. Loneliness is all over America; loneliness can be in our playground too. What will I do to bring the good news to the lonely?

Prayer of the faithful: Jesus, you knew loneliness as you suffered. Hear our prayers to you.

Response: Lord, hear us.

For those whose friends have all died or moved away, that they may discover someone who cares . . .
For a bigger share of Jesus in our lives, that he will always be our friend . . .
For someone at school who needs a friend, that we might reach out and say "Hi" . . .
For our special intentions, _____ we pray . . .

Offertory: Father, here is our gift of bread. While we have good bread to eat, others need a friend to feed them. Keep us mindful of them as we pray that this may become the bread of life.
Response: Blessed be God forever.

Father, we bring you wine also. It comes from grapes crushed like the lives of many people who need a friend. Make all men reach out to one another as we pray that this may become our spiritual drink.
Response: Blessed be God forever.

Prayer over gifts: Father we need the warm love of your Son, not only in our lives but in the lives of people all over the world. That is why we offer you these gifts through your Spirit. Amen.

Eucharistic rite: Father, in the beginning you said it was not good for man to be alone so you created a companion, woman. When people were in slavery you guided them into a community of hope. When darkness had been over the earth too long you sent the brightness of your Son. His message was one of light and life, and so for all the signs of friendship and hope we proclaim thanks as we say: Holy, Holy, Holy . . .

Father, we recall the words and deeds of Jesus that gathered the apostles and their friends into a community of love. We remember that community today as it continues in our pope, our bishop and our parish community. We recall especially that on the night Jesus died he took bread, said a blessing, offered it to his friends and said "This is my Body given for you." After supper he blessed the cup of wine and said "Take and drink of this, it is my Blood shed for you and your sins. Do this in memory of me." And so we are no longer alone. We have Jesus with us. The Spirit has been sent to gladden us and unite us and all men. Through Jesus and with him and in him we offer these gifts of his Body and Blood to you, Father with the Spirit forever and ever. Amen.

Response: All sing Amen using the "Yes, Amen" melody (Wise, World Library of Sacred Music).

Communion song: Play "Bridge Over Troubled Water (Simon and Garfunkel, Columbia).

Response: Let us think about some way we can help remove the loneliness of others:
- Bring a flower to someone.
- Befriend someone who is alone.
- Visit or write to a person who lives alone.
- Run errands for a lonely or helpless person.

Dismissal: As we close with our last blessing, let us reach out and hold hands with those next to us.

God our Father, thank you for your call. Jesus our brother stay with us as our Word. Holy Spirit, give joy to men through our lives. Amen.

Follow-up: Remind students of post-communion mediation or have a class "project against loneliness" each day of the coming week. Write letters to prisoners, servicemen; send a donation to the USO.

END OF THE SCHOOL YEAR: PICNIC OF PRAISE

Theme: One of the most common experiences is to celebrate the completion of a school year with a picnic. Every group seems to have one: patrol boys, servers, volleyball team, and graduating class. Here we celebrate such accomplishments in the context of sharing a picnic meal and the eucharist.

Materials and preparation:
- Site selection is important. Two areas—one for the word service and another for the eucharistic service should be prepared. The first site might be the place of departure while the second might be a clearing in the picnic area. Blankets should be used for seating.
- A flat top picnic basket should be prepared with bread and wine, stole, chalice, paten or plate and a large tray for the offerings.
- Each person brings his own lunch and a package of cookies to be presented at the offertory and shared later.
- Musical instruments could be brought for the liturgy as well as for a song session afterward.

Celebration introduction: Once the group gathers, share a few spontaneous comments on why we celebrate and how Jesus loved to celebrate with his friends (Cana, at the seashore, etc.). Then open with a simple "Peace be with you."

Penitential rite: During the year we often had misunderstandings. We may have been jealous or unkind. Or perhaps we were especially happy because of something another person did for us. As our rite of reconciliation, let us take a moment to go to another person and share our feelings, ask pardon and offer thanks to them.

Prayer: Spirit of God, thank you for the united spirit of our class and school. We offer this picnic of praise with Jesus our brother in thanks to you and the Father. Amen.

Reading I: Robert Frost's "The Mending Wall" or Isaiah 62:11-12.

Response: Allow members of the group to paraphrase Psalm 117.

Reading II: I Corinthians 13:4-13 (gifts of love).

Response: Silent meditation on this year's gifts.

Reading III: John 2:1-12 (feast at Cana).

Homily: God spoke to us through the readings we have heard. Now let us allow him to speak through our mouths as we comment on what we have heard, sharing our thoughts. *(Here the participants engage in a dialogue homily on their growth and change throughout the past year.)*

Procession: As we end our word service, we can express our joy in a friendly and relaxed procession to the picnic site. (The place for the actual picnic should be a comfortable and scenic place in the woods. As the procession arrives, blankets are spread out for everyone to be seated, including the celebrant. The large picnic basket will serve as the altar.)

Offertory: After all are settled, allow the participants to offer petitions, pass around a tray to collect the cookies (symbolic of the offering of ourselves).

Prayer over gifts: Jesus, "eucharist" means thanksgiving and today we want to tell you how grateful we are for the past school year with all its happy moments. We can think of no better way to do this than in the offering of this bread and wine through you to the Father. Amen.

Eucharistic prayer: Use any preface desired and follow with "Holy, Holy, Holy . . ."

Canon: Blessed are you Almighty God, Father of our Lord Jesus Christ. Blessed are you! You have chosen us and you have liberated us from the power of darkness and brought us into the kingdom of your beloved Son. He is the image of your glory, for in him the universe was made; in him we have received redemption and forgiveness for sins. On the night before he died he took bread, said a blessing, broke it, and gave it to his friends, saying, "Take and eat for this is my Body." Then he took the cup of wine and blessed it, saying, "Take and drink from this, for it is the cup of my Blood, shed for you and all men. Do this in memory of me." Therefore, Lord our God, we place here this sign of our faith. And today we commemorate his suffering and death, but most of all his victory over death. Glorified at your right hand, he speaks on our behalf. He will come to do justice to the living and dead on the day which you have appointed. We pray, Lord our God, send us your Holy Spirit—the Spirit who brings to life the power of Jesus Christ. We pray that this bread and this cup which we offer you in humility may really be the signs of our surrender to you. We pray that before the eyes of all people with whom we are united, we may live your Gospel and be the sign of your peace in this world. May we support and serve each other in love. May our hearts be opened to the poor, the sick and the dying and to all who are in need. We pray that we may be the Church of Jesus Christ united with our Pope _____, our Bishop _____ and with all believers everywhere on this earth. Through him and with him and in him you are blessed and praised, Lord God, Almighty Father, in union with the Holy Spirit, today and all days until eternity.

Response: Sing "Amen" ("Lilies of the Field").

Communion song:

- "Gonna Sing My Lord" (Wise, World Library of Sacred Music).
- "You Fill the Day" (Wise, World Library of Sacred Music).

Prayer: Holy Spirit, we know your power through the growth and joy we have felt during the past year. Keep all of us safe during the coming vacation and help us to live in loving service to others. Amen.

Dismissal: We now join in sharing our picnic food and the cookies we have offered. We know that Jesus is still with us and our friendship now continues to be the sign of his presence.

Follow-up: Send letters of thanks to the principal, cafeteria manager, janitors, and crossing guards. A personal visit by representatives from the group may be even more effective.

ADVENT: HEAR THE VOICE OF THE PROPHETS

Theme: The prophet is one who issues calls to new fidelity rather than simply foretelling the future. So often we criticize those who are false and deceive us. Let us pray over our own need to call ourselves and others to new honesty before the Lord who comes and will come again.

Materials and preparation:
- Prepare a "graffiti wall" of what a prophet might say to the people of today to urge them to prepare for Jesus. Use this as an antependium or backdrop to the altar.
- Dramatize several of the prophets speaking in contemporary terms. Father Montague's records "The Prophet's Dream," "Meet the Prophets," (Argus) and the Dameans' "New Creation" (FEL) are possible models.
- Discuss contemporary prophetic figures. Assemble "good news" clippings of such people.
- Another good resource is the seventh grade manual from the Allyn and Bacon religion series, offering suggestions for this particular topic.
- The Josephite Pastoral Center in Washington, D.C. offers a desk calendar of "modern prophets" which might offer insights, examples and ideas.

Celebration introduction: In preparing the world for the coming of Jesus God used prophets to show the way, "to go before." Jesus is reborn today in life and love. And God is still calling prophets—maybe you and me—to point out Jesus as John the Baptist did long ago. Let us hope we are ready to listen.

Entrance song: "King of Glory" (FEL). A guitar and tambourine add to this song.

Greeting: Prepare the way of the Lord; make straight his paths. *Response:* Every valley shall be filled and every mountain leveled and all men shall see the salvation of our God.

Penitential rite: For the times we didn't listen to your call we pray, Lord have mercy. For the times we said cruel words to others we pray, Christ have mercy. For the times we walked away from your work we pray, Lord have mercy.

Father, we want to hear your call today; we want to do your work in the world. Give us strength through Jesus and the Spirit. Amen.

Reading I: adapted from Jeremiah 1:6, 20:2, 37:15-16. Jeremiah was an ordinary citizen, one who would never have dreamed of being a leader in his country. But Yahweh called him and this shy, timid man answered yes. As he tells us, "The word of Yahweh was addressed to me saying,' . . . I have appointed you as prophet to the nations.' I said, 'Lord, Yahweh, I do not know how to speak—I am a child!' But Yahweh replied, 'Do not say, "I am a child." Do not be afraid of them, for I am with you to protect you . . .' "

It was hard to keep saying "yes." But Jeremiah tried and he soon learned that to live as a prophet and patriot was to risk suffering. He was beaten and then put in the stocks at the Gate of Benjamin. Repeatedly Jeremiah found himself in prison. Yet he kept trying and said "yes" to Yahweh's command until he was killed.

Reading II: *Call to Liberty and Greatness* (Allyn and Bacon), 1, p. 29, Joan of Arc. Three people should perform this in a dramatic reading.

Meditation: Psalm 22 (The Lord Is My Shepherd) using the Gelineau melody.

Reading III: Matthew 5:1-10 (the beatitudes).

Homily: We are all ordinary men like Jeremiah, called to be prophets. It is sometimes hard, as we see in Joan of Arc's experience. But Jesus promises us we will be fulfilled and happy.

Creed: I believe in God, the Father the creator who made all things and called men forth as the glory of his creation. I believe in Jesus who lived and died as man to give us new life, a new calling and who sends us as his prophets. I believe in the Spirit who breathed over the earth and who sends us forth in power today. Through the Church, the new people of God bear witness to the good news that man can live on. I believe in the resurrection and the union of all men with God forever. Amen.

Offering song: "Take Our Bread" (Jabusch, FEL).

Prayer over gifts: Father, take these gifts of bread and wine as a sign of our lives and our words bringing your good news to all men. We offer them through Jesus and the Spirit to you God, forever and ever. Amen.

Eucharistic prayer: Use canon 2.

Communion song: "You Are My People"

Response: Sometimes we think we are too young or too weak to be witnesses for Jesus. Just as he used the young boy's fish to feed the multitude, so too he can use us to spread the good news if we are ready and willing. As our closing prayer and response, let us renew our baptismal vows and tell the Lord we are ready!

Dismissal: Go now as prophets to love and serve the Lord.
Response: Thanks be to God.

Closing song: "Turn Your Eyes" (Ducote, FEL) or "Witness Song" (Blue, FEL).

Follow-up: Tell another person about the prophets mentioned in this liturgy. Have various members of the group search for modern prophets in their community. Film, interviews or written reports may be used to capture the nature of this "modern prophet" and present his or her work to the class.

CONFIRMATION: SPIRIT—THE SECRET INGREDIENT

Theme: "New, improved" is the story of the consumer's life today. The added dimension of the Spirit for the contemporary Christian is important. The life that begins in baptism and grows in eucharist is shown and shared with the world through the spirit of confirmation. The Spirit is "the secret ingredient" for a full life.

Materials and preparation:

- With younger students the use of helium balloons and/or bubble makers may enhance the celebration. Kite flying may be a possible illustration. The idea would be to demonstrate the need of a special force to propel a kite or a balloon and relate the Spirit as the force which builds on the foundation of baptism.
- Good "vocation type" films may form material for a homily. If the sacrament is administered in high school you should stress some of the elements found in the previous liturgy on prophets, i.e., confirmation makes us "priest and prophet."
- Discuss the value of team or school spirit. Have an essay contest or allow the participants to prepare an audio-visual presentation on the subject.

Celebration introduction: When we were tiny babies we couldn't talk. We couldn't even feed ourselves. Now, however, we can take care of ourselves and explain our needs to others. When we were in the third grade, we couldn't drive a car, but we now look forward to that responsibility. As baptized Christians we are growing to receive a new power into our lives—the love of the Spirit. We sing of that power.

Entrance song: "The Spirit Is A'Movin" (Landry, North American Liturgy Resources).

Greeting: May God our Father, Jesus our brother and the power and love of the Spirit be with you.
Response: And also with you.

Penitential rite: Each of us has been called to love others in a special way, but sometimes we are selfish, so we pray, Lord have mercy. Each of us has been given special talents, but sometimes we hide our gifts, so we pray, Christ have mercy. Each of us should be a sign of God's presence but sometimes we fail to speak, so we pray, Lord have mercy.

Prayer: Spirit of God, give us a deeper power of love and sacrifice. Help us show forth our special gifts and put your special strength in our hearts that we may be mature Christians now and forever. Amen.

Reading I: Acts 2:1-4.

Response: Have students hum "Spirit Is A'Movin."

Reading II: John 15:20-27.

Homily: Consider the amazing feats of people in crisis situations (e.g., courage to save a drowning child). A second breath gives a runner extra strength and belief in himself so he can score a touchdown. The Spirit adds new power to our lives if we let him.

Prayer of the faithful:

Response: Spirit of God, hear us.

That a cold world and cold people may be warmed with your love . . .
That we may be a light to our friends to show your power . . .
That our families may grow closer in serving each other . . .
That the sick and the dying may know your strength in their pain . . .
We pause to include our special intentions.

Offertory song: A traditional rendition of "Veni Creator Spiritus" or an English version could be used.

Prayer over gifts: Bread strengthens men's bodies and wine celebrates the joy in men's lives. Spirit of God, take these gifts, transform them into body and blood and change our lives through them. We ask this in the name of God the Father and Jesus our brother. Amen.

Eucharistic rite: Use the preface of the Holy Spirit and canon 4.

Communion rite: "Spirit of the Lord" (Ault, FEL).

Response: Have the parents/adult confirmed members of the parish community come forth to impose hands on those confirmed.

Prayer: Thank you, Holy Spirit, for the gentle power you give now that we have called Jesus into our lives. Keep us moving out to others in the world and toward you with Father and Son, forever and ever. Amen.

Closing song: "They'll Know We Are Christians" (Scholtes, FEL) or "New Creation" (Ault, FEL). Another option would be to have a procession out with trumpets playing joyful music.

Follow-up:
- Make a mini mobile or silk screen a banner to be used as a "confirmation certificate." Sample banner can be obtained from Rev. Sidney Becnel, Box 2108, Baton Rouge, La. 70821.

SAMPLE LITURGIES
SUITABLE FOR SENIOR HIGH SCHOOL

Life Themes:
- Creation: Ecology
- Relationships: Communication
- Festivals: Fourth of July

Liturgical Themes:
- Church Year: Easter
- Sacraments: Marriage

ECOLOGY: POLLUTION IS A DIRTY WORD!

Theme: The spirit of the times addresses itself to responsible Christian living. The relation between ecology and Christian concern for the beauties of creation allows us to celebrate our efforts to preserve our environment.

Materials and preparation:
- Many movies have been made to dramatize the problems of pollution. Check your state library film department or local health unit. Better yet—make your home movie or use slides of area problems.
- The site for the eucharist could be in an area where bottles, cans, or paper to be recycled is stored.
- Resolutions about our carelessness with nature could be incorporated into the liturgy. A good resource here is *Children's Liturgies*, Liturgical Conference, Washington, D.C., p. 198.

Celebration entrance: Play or sing "America the Beautiful" accompanied by slides of national parks, city monuments, etc.

Penitential rite: Use "Exorcisms of Earth, Air and Water Pollution" from *Children's Liturgies* by Virginia Sloyan and Gabe Huck, Liturgical Conference, Washington, D.C. 20070.

Opening prayer: Father, this day is your gift to us, filled with all the blessings of life, the good things of earth which come from your hands. We stand in wonder at all that you have given us, and ask what we can give you in return. All you ask of those you have called your sons is that our love for each other be real. May we now set aside all that is empty and shallow, all that condemns us to love on life's borders, that keeps us a distance from each other and from you. Help us to break through to that area of human life where men can touch each other in love, for there we will find what you say when you made us to be like you. All glory be to you, Father, now and forever (Rev. John Gallen, *Eucharistic Liturgies*, Paulist/Newman Press).

Reading I: Canticle of St. Francis to Creation.

Be praised, my Lord, with all your created things.
Be praised for brother sun who brings the day and gives us light.
He is fair and radiant with a shining face and he draws his meaning from on high.
Be praised, my Lord, for sister moon and the stars in the heavens. You have made them clear and precious and lovely.
Be praised, my Lord, for our brother wind, and for the air and clouds and calm days and every kind of weather by which you give your creatures nourishment.
Be praised, my Lord, for our sister water, which is very helpful and humble and precious and pure.
Be praised, my Lord, for our brother fire, by which you light up the darkness; he is fair and mighty and strong.
Be praised, my Lord, for our mother earth, for she sustains and keeps us and brings forth all kinds of fruits together with the grasses and the bright flowers.
Be praised, my Lord, for our sister bodily death, from which no living man can flee. Be praised, my Lord, for all creatures. Amen.

Response: Psalm 148:3-14.

Reading II: Selection on the elements from *Elements of Hope* (Paulist/Newman Press, Paramus, N.J.).

Meditation: Silence or play the record "Morning Has Broken" (Cat Stevens, North American Publishers Corp., Hialeah, Fla.).

Reading III: Genesis I.

Homily: Do we really "give a damn?" Everybody's problem is often nobody's problem. Some statistics from the local Sierra Club are effective in presenting ecological balance. Scripture tells us about our "stewardship" or duty to the world around us.

Offertory procession and prayer of the faithful: Participants bring the objects described below and place them in a large trash can near the altar.

Response: Hear us, O Lord.

(*As a crumpled piece of paper is disposed of*) That we may become more conscious of the value of a tree . . .

(*As a few bottles are disposed of*) That we may be more conscious of the beauty of sand . . .
(*As cans are added*) That we may preserve the precious ores of the earth . . .
(*As a baby doll is pitched in*) That we may protect the right of the unborn and yet to be conceived . . .
(*As bread is offered*) That we who are filled with food may be aware of those who hunger . . .
(*As wine is offered*) That we whose lives are gladdened with wine will not forget the plight of the migrant . . .

Prayer over gifts: Father, if we do not care for our earth, it will no longer be able to offer food for our sustenance. We are glad to offer this bread and wine as a pledge that we will care for all creation. We offer it in Jesus' name. Amen.

Eucharistic prayer: Blessed are you, Lord, for the air we breathe. Thanks to you, Lord, for the earth that feeds us. Blessed are you, Lord, for the fire that warms. Thanks to you Lord, for the water that quenches our thirst. And so with all of creation, the angels and all the saints we praise you as we say: Holy, Holy, Holy . . .

Use canon 2.

Communion Song: "For the Beauty of the Earth" (Virgil Ford *Sing and Tell*, Broadman Press, Nashville, Tennessee.)

Response: Project slides with soft background music while someone reads the following:
William Wordsworth sees a reflection of men in nature: ". . . For I have learned to look on nature, not as in the hour of thoughtless youth, but hearing often times the still, sad music of humanity." Lord Byron admired the ocean for its freedom and supremacy: ". . . Roll on, thou deep and dark blue ocean, roll! Ten thousand fleets sweep over in vain—man marks the earth with ruin; his control stops with the shore." Samuel Taylor Coleridge, in his poem "The Rime of the Ancient Mariner," showed a unity of all of creation: ". . . He prayeth best, who loveth best. All things both great and small; For the dear God who loveth us, He made and loveth all." Gerard Manley Hopkins saw in nature the grandeur of God: "The world is charged with the grandeur of God. It will flame out like shining shook foil; It gathers to a greatness, like the ooze of oil crushed." Henry David Thoreau wrote the wonder of nature: ". . . The philosopher for whom rainbows can be explained away never saw them."

Prayer: Father, take the power of transformation which has made bread and wine into body and blood and transform our weakness and destructive power into strength to recreate the earth. We ask this in Jesus' name. Amen.

Dismissal song: "This is the Day" (Blue, FEL).

Follow-up: Have each participant do one of the following:
- Wear a "Give a Damn" button or "Celebrate Life" button.
- Clean his desk, classroom, and bedroom.
- Research and present a project on the recycling of paper or glass or cans. Put the report into action with a campaign.
- Present a slide show on Ecology at the next home and school association meeting.

COMMUNICATION: SOUNDS OF SILENCE

Theme: The life of Jesus was the Father's great attempt at dialog with creation. Jesus touched many as the Word and brought life and light to all men. We labor to extend that good news but are often tempted to be silent and break off communications. This liturgy celebrates man's need to communicate with others.

Materials and preparation:
- The liturgy up to the canon may be held the single light of the Paschal candle or it may begin just before sunrise out of doors.
- As part of the liturgy of the word, a sound collage might be assembled to be listened to in darkness. Include "Richard Cory," "Nowhere Man" (Beatles) and "Sounds of Silence" (Simon and Garfunkel) and other pop songs which illustrate a lack of communication.
- Check the catalogue of Teleketics films for appropriate visuals (1229 South Santee, Los Angeles, California).
- A charade-type pantomine of silence and failure to communicate could add to the theme in homily.
- Each person might prepare some small, handmade gift to be shared with another.

Celebration introduction: Read John 1:1-5 ("In the beginning . . ."

Entrance song: Play a record of "Sounds of Silence" from album of the same name by Simon and Garfunkel. Another selection from the same album is "I Am a Rock."

Penitential rite: Each of us is sometimes an island. Each feels totally self-sufficient. Yet man hallucinates and often goes insane, as scientists tell us, when left totally alone. We pause to think of our selfishness and our aloofness (*pause*). We reach out and touch another in reconciliation and hope. (*Pause for participants to turn to one another.*)

Opening prayer: Spontaneous expression, perhaps reflecting on recent events of non-communication.

Reading I: Selection from the poetry of Rod McKuen or the words to "Sounds of Silence" or "I Am a Rock."

Reading II: John 13:1-20 or Romans 13:11-13.

Homily: Reflect together and dialog on the importance of communication. *(Note: at this point more lights are added.)*

Prayer of the faithful: This may be recited by leader and group or by alternating sides of the congregation.

Response: Lord, you call to me, and I give no reply.

When I see the hungry and feed them not . . .
When public servants go unappreciated . . .
When I refuse to recognize that another is in pain . . .
When I turn my back upon my brother of a different race . . .
When I do not try to bridge the generation gap . . .
When I fail to care about the lonely people of the world . . .
When I fail to comfort the sick . . .
(Silent meditation)

Offertory: Simply offer bread and wine in silent prayer.

Priest: Lift up your hearts.
All: We lift them to the Lord.
Priest: Let us give thanks for God's glory.
All: We give thanks; we rejoice in the glory of all creation.
Priest: All glory be to you, O Father, who sent your only Son into the world to be a man, born of a woman's womb, to die for us on a cross that was made by us.
All: He came for us. Help us to accept his coming.
Priest: A man, he walked among us on our earth, in our world of conflict, and commanded us to remember his death which gives us life and to wait for him until he comes again in glory.
All: We remember his death; we live by his presence and we wait for his coming.
Priest: On the night he was betrayed, the Lord Jesus took bread; he gave thanks. He broke it and gave it to his disciples, saying, "Take, eat, this is my Body." He also took the cup and gave thanks. He gave it to them saying, "Drink of it, all of you; this is my Blood of the covenant which is poured out for many for the forgiveness of sins. Do this in remembrance of me."

All: Come, Lord Jesus, come.

Priest: Therefore, remembering his death, believing in his rising from the grave, longing to recognize his presence, now in this place, we obey his command. We offer bread and wine; we offer ourselves to be used in his work of love.

All: Everything is yours, O Lord; we return the gift which you first gave us.

Priest: Accept it, Father. Send down the Spirit of life and power, glory and love, upon these people, upon this bread and wine (*here the celebrant may extend his hands over the bread and wine*), that to us they may be his Body and Blood.

All: Come, risen Lord, live in us that we may live in you.

Priest: Now with all men who ever were, are and will be, with all creation in all time, with joy we say:

All: Holy, Holy, Holy Lord God Almighty, all space and all time show forth your glory now and always. Amen.

Priest: And now, in his words we are bold to say: (The Lord's Prayer).

Communion song: "Sign of Total Giving," (Ault, FEL).

Response: Pause to give the small, handmade gift to the person next to you or think of someone lonely or someone to whom you owe a letter and make a resolution concerning him/her.

Prayer: Jesus, you used bread and wine to communicate your great love and desire for union with us. Help us to communicate with each other and spread your good news. Amen.

Dismissal: As lights are extinguished, play "Bridge Over Troubled Water" (Simon and Garfunkel) or sing "Turn Your Eyes" (Ducote, FEL).

Follow-up:
- If a gift was not shared after communion, do so after mass.
- Make and present candles for the altar.
- Write a letter to someone you have almost forgotten.

FOURTH OF JULY:
A CELEBRATION OF FREEDOM'S PROMISES

Theme: We are certainly grateful for the freedoms we enjoy as Christians and Americans. Yet we are aware that freedom sometimes promises more than it can deliver and it includes a call to responsibility. This celebration touches the fulfilled and unfulfilled elements of freedom's challenge.

Materials and preparation:
- A mobile could be the focal point above the altar. Hang pictures on it which illustrate freedom fulfilled and unfulfilled.
- As the worshippers enter the room their hands are tied together with a piece of gauze or other similar binding (bow on top). This is released by another at the peace greeting.
- A large American flag collage could be constructed with the stars and stripes representing various areas of freedom fulfilled and denied.

Celebration introduction: As we near the celebration of the 200th anniversary of our nation's founding, we recall that each man in every generation from then until now has sought to redefine for himself the reality of freedom. Many of us still struggle to see it fulfilled. The Constitution echoes St. Paul's statement that we are free sons of God and yet we agonize over its unfulfilled potential.

Entrance song: "Star Spangled Banner" from *Woodstock* album or "Preamble to the Constitution" by the Fifth Dimension.

Penitential rite: For not making the good news of the gospel and the freedom that is ours a real part of our lives, we pray, Lord have mercy, Christ have mercy, Lord have mercy.

For not seeing the beauty of others nor helping them to discover their talents, we pray, Lord have mercy, Christ have mercy, Lord have mercy.

(Add other statements as desired.)

Opening prayer: Father, we know how easy it is to deny freedom—our own and others'. May we set a new standard of hope and fulfill the potential that lies ahead. We ask this through the strength of your Spirit, God forever and ever. Amen.

Reading I: Select a reading from contemporary freedom literature of such writers as Martin Luther King, Jerry Rubin, Bob Dylan.

Reading II: Galatians 4:1-7 (bondage and freedom).

Meditation: Use the prayer of St. Francis of Assisi "Lord, make me an instrument of your peace . . ."

Reading III: Luke 24:13-35 (The Liberator lived among us).

Homily: Are you a slave or free man? Does Christ's liberation of men find reality in your life? Does freedom require laws? Help others to be free also!

Prayer of the faithful: Heavenly Father, each person you create is a mystery to be discovered. Help us to know how to live our life in a discovering way.

Response: We pray to the Lord.

For all the leaders in the Church, that they may help the people in their care to be discoverers of all that God gives them . . .
For those who must discover the best way to serve the community . . .
For everyone here, that we may help each other to discover all the gifts that our heavenly Father has given to us . . .
For all those in need of discovering their true selves, that the Holy Spirit may guide them in new growth and understanding . . .
We now add our own intentions.

Offertory song: "Come Away" (Repp, FEL), or "New Creation" (Ault, FEL).

Prayer over gifts: Father, accept these gifts and help us to live the freedom that they proclaim to us as Sons of God and brothers of Jesus. We ask this through your Spirit. Amen.

Eucharistic rite (Preface): Father, you promised Adam victory over Satan. You led the Israelites out of bondage. You freed David from Goliath's grip. You gave Elizabeth a child in her old age. Your Son came to free us from evil and call us as his brothers and sisters.

He sent the Spirit to empower us to live in love. For your constant favor we join all creation in saying: Holy, Holy, Holy . . .

Follow with canon 3.

At the time of the peace greeting, if the hands were tied upon entry, each person should *free* his neighbor wishing him "peace."

Communion song: "Come Away" (Repp, FEL). If time permits, play either "Born Free" (Bary and Black) or "If I Had a Hammer" (Peter, Paul and Mary).

Response: Freedom doesn't necessarily mean a lack of laws or rules. Let us pause to think of a law or rule that we need to strengthen or reaffirm our belief in.

Prayer: Have representative students offer a closing prayer of thanks.

Dismissal: Matthew 5:3-10 or Luke 6:20-23 (the beatitudes).

Follow-up: Visit the police station/county jail and sympathetically try to understand the problems of police and prisoners. Read up on the plight of U.S. migrant workers or Indians and report in an audio-visual presentation to the class. Discover the programs of the local antipoverty program, ACLU, Campaign for Human Development and implement one program into your parish.

EASTER: SEARCH FOR FAITH IN THE RISEN LORD

Theme: To move from adolescence to adulthood often involves deep trauma physically, psychologically, and spiritually. Here we celebrate the struggle of a maturing person to come to grips with the question of faith. We reflect today on the struggle of those closest to Jesus to do the same.

Materials and preparation:
- A slide-tape presentation could be prepared emphasizing the theme of search for faith. (One approach would be a comparison with the search for a cure for cancer, for oil, for life on the moon.)
- Have each person bring a record or a quote that deals with the question of "search."

Celebration introduction: Evening, Thomas, be strong, fear not! Welcome to the search. Throughout the pages of history man has confronted the meaning of Jesus—a confrontation that has been long and tortuous, filled with hills and valleys, heights and depths. And yet history remains young in the search and today's teen even younger!

Evening, Thomas, be strong, fear not! It is a search for the meaning of Christ in our lives—our search for a living faith—that we celebrate. Some people have found Jesus and hoard him in the depths of their being, fearful of sharing the good news, hiding their piece of Jesus from risk—a fear of loss perhaps, but never experiencing possibilities of great growth. Others fling him carelessly about, using their claim to his name in vain, abusing him once more in history, never having the honesty to discard their unfair claim to his name. Others, maybe you, still search honestly, wanting to risk, to abandon themselves, afraid alone . . . Evening, Thomas, be strong, fear not! Let's celebrate your search.

Entrance: Use the audio-visual presentation suggested in "materials and preparation."

Greeting: We begin our reflection of our search for faith by a mini-profession: In the name of the Father, and of the Son and of the Holy Spirit. Amen.

Penitential rite: Father, we have mixed feelings about independence and dependence. We know you love us and yet we sometimes reject your love, so we pray, Lord have mercy. Jesus, you are our brother. Yet sometimes we want to be away from brothers and sisters to try to find ourselves, so we pray, Christ have mercy. Spirit, what an elusive person you can be. How often we feel hope and despair all mixed together, so we pray, Lord have mercy.

Prayer: Let's pause for a moment to focus on our own feelings about God and be open to possibilities of faith and search.

Reading I: "What Is Real?" selection from *The Velveteen Rabbit* by Margery Williams (New York: Doubleday).

Meditation: Play the song "I Don't Know How To Love Him" from the album *Jesus Christ Superstar*.

Reading II: Acts 5:12-16.

Meditation: "God Has Spoken to His People" (Wise, WLSM).

Reading III: John 20:19-31.

Homily: Unless we have *doubt* we cannot speak of faith. The experience of coming to identify our struggle, becoming a member of a community, can help us find ourselves. We can grow especially in sharing meals. "They recognized him in the breaking of bread."

Prayer of the faithful: Paraphrase the baptismal profession of faith. The response might be: I struggle to believe; help me, O Lord.

Offering song: We want to offer our search. Incomplete, questioning, and hesitant we come as best we can and we sing, "All That We Have" (Dameans, FEL).

Prayer over gifts: Jesus, we hesitate to speak to you, much less to put our lives on the line with you in this offering of bread and wine. But we know you were once man and therefore understand our search, so we say thanks and offer these gifts. Amen.

Eucharistic rite: Choose any preface and canon.

Communion song: Jesus shares in our search as he comes to us in the sign of bread and wine. We ask for strength in our struggle as we sing: "Look Beyond" (Ducote, FEL).

Response: (Provide pencils and paper for the participants.) For our post-communion meditation and prayer let us spend a minute writing about our struggle for faith, about our attempts to experience Jesus as the early Christians did. Let us write our own "good news" today. *(Pause about five minutes.)*

Now keep that revelation in your purse, wallet or scrapbook. Pray it often, share it with others as you wish. The apostles, after three years said, "Lord show us the Father." Thomas said, "Unless I put my hand into his side . . ." Gibran said, "In my heart dwells Jesus of Galilee, a man above men." Everly said, "Men have been so wrong about God that he had to come and tell them who he was." Carlyle said, "If Jesus Christ were to come today, people would not crucify him. They would ask him to dinner and hear what he had to say and make fun of it." T. S. Eliot said, "He is the still point of the turning world." Chardin said, "Christ is the terminal point at which the consummation of humanity is destined to be achieved." Shaw said, "You see things as they are and you ask why. I dream of things that never were and ask why not." Don Quixote said, "To dream the impossible dream . . ." Scripture said, "Alive, as he promised!" and "Be born again." Maybe you still say honestly, "I'm searching." Right on!

Dismissal: Now we go forth to continue our search by loving and serving others. We sing: "Turn Your Eyes" (Ault, FEL) or "Yes, Lord" (Ducote, FEL) or play the record "Both Sides Now" (Joni Mitchell, Reprise Records).

Follow-up:
- Those who wish may share the post-communion meditations; make them into a "prayerbook" for each person. Look up other quotes to include.
- Plan an hour of prayer later in the semester. Invite a group similar to the Dameans (for high school) or Joe Wise (for college) to perform or create your own musical group.

MARRIAGE: I DO, I DO?

Theme: Much is being spoken and written about values relating to marriage today. Changing patterns of family and social life call for a Christian response. A study of marriage as an institution and the sacrament of matrimony should lead to a celebration of the Christian vocation of marriage.

Materials and preparation:

- The homily could best be given by a realistic Christian married couple (mixed religions) together with reflections by a priest.
- Many visuals can be used. Among these would be the filmstrip "Eucharist, Covenant of Friendship" (Tom S. Klise Co., P.O. Box 3418, Peoria, Ill. 61614) which nicely compares the eucharist and the wedding commitment. The movie "We Do, We Do" (Franciscan Productions, 1229 So. Santee, Los Angeles, Cal.) illustrates some questions and challenges faced by young couples today.
- Perhaps parents of the teens could be invited to renew their marriage vows before their children.

Celebration introduction: We hear all kinds of things about love. People encourage us to all kinds of experimentation. "Try it, you'll like it" they say, and indeed marriage can be a great love affair if we liken it to God's love for us, Christ's love for the Church.

Entrance song: "We've Only Just Begun" (Carpenters).

Penitential rite: How can we love God whom we cannot see if we don't love our neighbor whom we see? For our failing to be people of prayer, our failing to respect one another and for our failure to love ourselves properly, we pray, Lord have mercy, Christ have mercy, Lord have mercy.

Glory to God and peace to his people. Father, for your faith in giving man and woman a share in your creative powers, we praise you. For helping us to know your love by our experience of each other, we bless you. For giving us marriage to build the earth and fulfill ourselves, we glorify you. Lord Jesus, for choosing to come among us through the institution of marriage and family life, we thank you. For working your first wondrous deed at a marriage feast and continuing to be with us through your sacramental presence in matrimony, we honor your name. Spirit of God, fill our lives with your love and sanctify our parents and all married people. Unite us now in your church to love and bring us all into unity with you, Christ and the Father forever. Amen.

Opening prayer: Let us pause to offer our experience of love to the Father in Jesus' name.

Reading I: Selections from *The Prophet*, Gibran (Knopf, N.Y.) or *The Art of Loving*, Fromm (Harper and Row, N.Y.)

Response: Sing Psalm 127 (Gelineau, Gregorian Institute of America, Toledo, Ohio)

Reading II: 1 Cor. 13.

Meditation: Play a recording or sing "Love Is Patient" (Baker, FEL).

Reading III: John 2:1-12 (wedding feast at Cana).

Homily: Few experiences of man have had more words written about them. The richness of marriage is elusive yet tangible through shared experiences. There is a need for idealism, in love of man and wife/Christ and church. Jesus is there to help.

Prayer of the faithful: Have the students or their parents compose the intentions or use statements from the literature suggested for readings followed by the response: Hear us, O Lord.

Offertory song: "Of My Hands" (Ray Repp, FEL).

Prayer over gifts: Bread and wine, wedding bands, newborn babies are all signs of love, of presence. Come, Lord Jesus, into our offerings and make them acceptable by joining them to your gift of love. Amen.

Eucharistic rite: Use the preface from the nuptial mass and canon 3.

Communion rite: Play the song "Close To You" (Carpenters).

Sing "Love Is Almost Worth the Dying" (Dameans, FEL).

Response: Let us show our love for Christ in each other as we greet one another in peace. *(Married couples could use this time to embrace and renew marriage vows.)*

Prayer: Spirit of love, come into our lives. Help us to be more conscious of the creative power of love that the Father shares with us and bring us one day into union with you for all eternity. Amen.

Dismissal: "They'll Know We Are Christians" (Scholtas, FEL).

Follow-up:
- Plan to visit with an elderly couple and enjoy their reminiscing about past experiences and love.
- Invite a marriage counselor to speak to the class.
- Give a prize for the freshest, most unusual suggestion of how one might express love to spouse/friend.

APPENDIX

SUGGESTED THEMES FOR LITURGIES

Primary

Advent: Luke 1:26, Luke 2:1-30.
Anger: Gen. 49:7, Prov. 14:17, Prov. 15:1.
Animals: Gen. 1:24-25, Gen. 2:19, Gen. 6:19, Luke 10:19.
Baptism: Mark 1:4, Luke 7:29, Acts 1:5, Acts 2:38, 1 Cor. 12:13, Matt. 28:19.
Bible: Deut. 31:26, Matt. 22:29, Mark 13:31, John 20:31.
Birthdays: Gen. 40:20, Matt. 14:6.
Brotherhood: Matt. 5:16, Matt. 7:12, Luke 6:36, Eph. 4:32, 1 John 4:7.
Charity: Matt. 13:31, Luke 17:3, 1 Cor. 13:1, 1 Pet. 4:8.
Choices, decisions: Deut. 30:19, 1 Cor. 15:58, Gal. 6:9, Ps. 32:8-11.
Creation: Gen. 1:26-28, Luke 11:5-8.
Discovery: Rev. 21:1-4, John 1:9-14.
Epiphany: Matt. 2:1-16.
Eucharist: Matt. 26:17-30, Mark 14:22-24, Luke 22:19-20, John 13:1-4.
Faith: Ps. 5:11, Ps. 7:1, Ps. 118:8-9, Matt. 15:28, Mark 9:23, Luke 17:6, John 3:16.
Family life: Gen. 18:19, Eph. 5:22-24.
Fatherhood: Hebrews 12:7-9, Luke 10:21-23.
Food: Gen. 9:3, Ps. 103:5, Matt. 6:11.
Forgiveness/reconciliation: Ex. 23:4, Prov. 19:11, Prov. 24:17, Matt. 5:7, Matt. 18:21, Mark 11:25, Luke 6:35, Rom. 12:14, 1 Cor. 4:12.
Friendship: Ps. 41:9, Ps. 55:12, Prov. 11:13, Prov. 17:9.
Gifts: Ps. 21:2, Ps. 34:10, Ps. 84:11, Eccl. 2:26, Matt. 11:28, Rom. 6:23, Rom. 8:32, Rom. 12:6-9.
Halloween and All Saints: Rom. 8:31-37, Rev. 7:24, John 3:1-3.
Happiness: Matt. 5:1-12, Luke 6:20-23, Is. 12:2-3, Job 5:17.
Heaven: Matt. 5:3, Matt. 6:20, John 14:2-3, Rev. 21:1-25.
Honesty: Deut. 25:13-16, 1 Thess. 4:11-12.
Light: Ps. 27:1, Ps. 119:105, Matt. 5:14, John 1:4.
Love: Deut. 6:5, Ps. 73:25-26, Lev. 19:18, 1 Cor. 13:4-8.
Motherhood: Ex. 20:12, Prov. 1:8, Prov. 10:1, Prov. 15:20.
Obeying: Ex. 19:5, John 10:27, John 14:15, Acts 5:29, John 5:3.
Parents: Hebrews 12:5-13, Luke 2:41-50.
Patriotism: Matt. 5:1-10; Jer. 1:6, Jer. 20:2, Jer. 37:15-16.

Peace: Ps. 133:1, Prov. 15:17, Prov. 20:3, Matt. 5:9, 1 Cor. 14:33.
Pentecost: Acts 2:2-4, Acts, 4:8, John 14:16.
Poverty: Prov. 15:16, Prov. 24:33-34.
Prayer: Luke 11:2-4, Matt. 6:5-15.
Recreation: Mark 6:31, Mark 7:24.
Responsibility: Luke 21:1-4, John 15:22-24, Matt. 12:41.
Teachers: Solomon 6:12-20, Luke 20:20-26.
Thanksgiving: Matt. 14:32-39, Ps. 50:14, Ps. 106:l, 1 Thess. 5:18.
Truth: Ps. 51:6, Ps. 89:14, Ps. 100:5, Prov. 12:19, John 14:6, John 16:13.

Intermediate

Advent: Luke 1:26, Luke 2:1-30.
Angels: Is. 6:2, Acts 12:7, Matt. 24:31.
Anger: Gen. 49:7, Prov. 14:17, Prov. 15:1.
Animals: Gen. 1:24-25, Gen. 2:19, Gen. 6:19, Luke 10:19.
Anointing of the sick: James 5:13-18.
Ascension: Ps. 47:5, Ps. 68:18, Mark 16:19.
Baptism: Mark 1:4, Luke 7:29, Acts 1:5, Acts 2:38, 1 Cor. 12:13, Matt. 28:19.
Bible: Deut. 31:26, Josh. 1:8, Matt. 22:29, Mark 13:31, John 20:31.
Birthdays: Gen. 40:20, Matt. 14:6.
Borrowing: Ex. 22:14, Ps. 37:21, Prov. 22:7.
Brotherhood: Matt. 5:16, Matt. 7:12, Luke 6:36, Eph. 4:32, 1 John 4:7.
Character: Prov. 22:1.
Charity: Matt. 18:21, Luke 17:3, 1 Cor. 13:1, 1 Pet. 4:8.
Choices, decisions: Deut. 30:19, 1 Cor. 15:58, Gal. 6:9, Heb. 11:24, Ps. 32:8-11.
Communism: Acts 2:44, Acts 4:32-37, Acts 5:1-2.
Courage: Prov. 28:1, Ezek. 3:9, 1 Cor. 16:13, 2 Tim. 1:7.
Creation: Gen. 1:26-28, Luke 11:5-8.
Discovery: Rev. 21:1-4, John 1:9-14.
Dishonesty: Lev. 6:2-7, Prov. 3:27.
Epiphany: Matt. 2:1-16.
Eucharist: Matt. 26:17-30, Mark 14:22-24, Luke 22:19-20, John 13:1-4, 1 Cor. 11:23-32, Acts 20:7.
Excuses: Gen. 3:12-13, Ex. 32:22, Acts 24:25.
Faith: Ps. 5:11, Ps. 7:1, Ps. 118:8-9, Matt. 15:28, Mark 9:23, Luke 17:6, John 3:16.
Family life: Gen. 18:19, Eph. 5:22-24.
Fatherhood: Hebrews 12:7-9, Luke 10:21-23.
Forgiveness/reconciliation: Ex. 23:4, Prov. 19:11, Prov. 24:17, Prov. 25:2, Matt. 5:7, Matt. 18:21, Mark 11:25, Luke 6:35, Rom. 12:14, 1 Cor. 4:12.
Freedom: John 8:31-38.

Friendship: Ps. 41:9, Ps. 55:12, Prov. 11:13, Prov. 17:9, Prov. 18:24.
Gifts: Ps. 21:2, Ps. 34:10, Ps. 84:11, Eccl. 2:26, Matt. 11:28, Rom. 6:23, Rom. 8:32, Rom. 12:6-8.
Gossip: Lev. 19:16, Prov. 11:13, Ps. 50:20.
Halloween and All Saints: Rom. 8:31-37, Rev. 7:24, Rev. 9:14, John 3:1-3.
Happiness: Matt. 5:1-12, Luke 6:20-23, Is. 12:2-3, Job 5:17.
Heaven: Deut. 26:15, Matt. 5:3, Matt. 6:20, John 14:2-3, Rev. 21:1-25.
Honesty: Lev. 19:35-36, Deut. 25:13-16, 1 Thess. 4:11-12.
Hospitality: Ex. 22:11, Lev. 19:10, Lev. 24:22, Luke 14:12, Heb. 13:2.
Life: Ps. 90:9, John 11:25-26, John 20:31.
Laws and rules: Hebrews 13:17-19, Matt. 22:34-40.
Light: Ps. 27:1, Ps. 119:105, Matt. 5:14, John 1:4.
Love: Deut. 6:5, Ps. 73:25-26, Lev. 19:18, 1 Cor. 13:4-8, 13.
Money: Jer. 17:11, Job 31:24-25, Luke 16:8-15, Matt. 19:21-26.
Motherhood: Ex. 20:12, Prov. 1:8, Prov. 10:1, Prov. 15:20, Prov. 29:15.
Obeying: Ex. 19:5, John 10:27, John 14:15, Acts 5:29, John 5:3.
Parents: Hebrews 12:5-13, Luke 2:41-50.
Patience: Heb. 10:36.
Patriotism: Matt. 5:1-10, Jer. 1:6, Jer. 20:2, Jer. 37:15-16.
Peace: Ps. 133:1, Prov. 15:17, Prov. 20:3, Matt. 5:9, 1 Cor. 14:33, Col. 1:2.
Pentecost: Acts 2:2-4, Acts 4:8, John 14:16.
Poverty: Prov. 15:16, Prov. 24:33-34.
Prayer: Luke 11:2-4, Matt. 6:5-15.
Recreation: Mark 6:31, 32, Mark 7:24.
Responsibility: Luke 21:1-4, John 15:22-24, Matt. 12:41.
Salvation: Ex. 15:2, John 3:14-17, John 5:24.
Teachers: Solomon 6:12-20, Luke 20:20-26.
Thanksgiving: Matt. 14:32-39, Ps. 50:14, Ps. 105:1, 1 Thess. 5:18.
Time: Ps. 90:8-10, Rom. 13:11-12, John 16:16.
Truth: Ps. 51:6, Ps. 89:14, Ps. 100:5, Prov. 12-19, John 14:6, John 16:13.

Junior and Senior High

Advent: Luke 1:26, Luke 2:1-30.
Alcohol: Is. 5:11, Eph. 5:18, Rom. 13:13.
Angels: Is. 6:2, Acts 12:7, Matt. 24:31.
Anger: Gen. 49:7, Prov. 14:17, Prov. 15:1.
Animals: Gen. 1:24-25, Gen. 2:19, Gen. 6:19, Luke 10:19.
Anointing of the sick: James 5:13-18.
Ascension: Ps. 47:5, Ps. 68:18, Mark 16:19.
Astrology: Is. 47:13, Jer. 10:1-2, Dan. 1:20, Dan. 2:27, Dan. 4:7.
Baptism: Mark 1:4, Luke 7:29, Acts 1:5, Acts 2:38, 1 Cor. 12:13, Matt. 28:19.

Bible: Deut. 31:26, Josh. 1:8, Matt. 22:29, Mark 13:31, John 20:31.
Birthdays: Gen. 40:20, Matt. 14:6.
Borrowing: Ex. 22:14, Ps. 37:21, Prov. 22:7.
Brotherhood: Matt. 5:16, Matt. 7:12, Luke 6:36, Eph. 4:32, John 4:7.
Character: Prov. 22:1.
Charity: Matt. 18:21, Luke 17:3, 1 Cor. 13:1, 1 Pet. 4:8.
Choices, decisions: Deut. 30:19, 1 Cor. 15:58, Gal. 6:9, Ps. 32:8-11.
Communism: Acts 2:44, Acts, 4:32-37, Acts 5:1-2.
Confidence: Ps. 20:7, Prov. 3:5.
Conscience: Job 27:6, Matt. 6:22, John 3:20.
Conversation: Eph 4:29, Col. 3:8, Col. 4:6.
Courage: Prov. 28:1, Ezek. 3:9, 1 Cor. 16:13, 2 Tim. 1:7.
Creation: Gen. 1:26-28, Luke 11:5-8.
Dancing: Ex. 15:20, Ex. 32:19, 2 Sam. 6:14, Ps. 149:3.
Death: Dan. 12:2, Rom. 5:12, 1 Cor. 15:21, Ps. 23, 1 Cor. 15:51-57.
Discovery: Rev. 21:1-4, John 1:9-14
Dishonesty: Lev. 6:2-7, Prov. 3:27.
Drugs: Rom. 13:11-14, Gal. 5:16-24, 1 Cor. 9:24-27, Matt. 24:45-51, Luke 21:34-36.
Epiphany: Matt. 2:1-16.
Eucharist: Matt. 26:17-30, Mark 14:22-24, Luke 22:19-20, John 13:1-4, 1 Cor. 11:23-32, Acts 20:7.
Excuses: Gen. 3:12-13, Ex. 32:22, Acts. 24:25.
Faith: Ps. 5:11, Ps. 7:1, Ps. 118:8-9, Mark 9:23, Luke 17:6, John 3:16.
Family life: Gen. 18:19, Eph. 5:22-24.
Fatherhood: Hebrews 12:7-9, Luke 10:21-23.
Fear: Ex. 20:18, Deut. 5:29, Job. 28:28, Ps. 23, Phil. 4:19, 2 Tim. 2:19.
Forgiveness/reconciliation: Ex. 23:4, Prov. 19:11, Prov. 24:17, Prov. 25:2, Matt. 5:7, Matt. 18:21, Mark 11:25, Luke 6:35, Rom. 12:14, 1 Cor. 4:12.
Freedom: John 8:31-38.
Friendship: Ps. 41:9, Ps. 55:12, Prov. 11:13, Prov. 17:9, Prov. 18:24.
Gifts: Ps. 21:2, Ps. 34:10, Ps. 84:11, Eccl. 2:26, Matt. 11:28, Rom. 6:23, Rom. 8:32, Rom. 12:6-8.
Gossip: Lev. 19:16, Prov. 11:13, Ps. 50:20.
Halloween and All Saints: Rom. 8:31-37, Rev. 7:24, Rev. 9:14, John 3:1-3.
Happiness: Matt. 5:1-12, Luke 6:20-23, Is. 12:2-3, Job 5:17.
Hatred: Lev. 19:17, Prov. 10:12, Prov. 15:27, Matt. 5:43-44, John 17:14, 1 John 2:9.
Heaven: Deut. 26:15, Matt. 5:3, Matt. 6:20, John 14:2-3, Rev. 21:1-25.
Hope: Ps. 31:24, Ps. 33:18, Ps. 39:7, Ps. 43:5, Ps. 71:5, Col. 1:5, 1 Peter 3:15.
Hospitality: Ex. 22:21, Lev. 19:10, Lev. 24:22, Deut. 10:18, Deut. 27:19,

Luke 14:12, Heb. 13:2.
Humility: Prob. 27:2, Rom. 12:3, 1 Cor. 3:8.
Jealousy/envy: Prov. 23:17, Song 8:6.
Judgment: Matt. 16:27, Matt. 25:41, Rev. 1:7, 1 Cor. 3:8.
Life: Ps. 90:9, John 11:25-26, John 20:31.
Laws and rules: Hebrews 13:17-19, Matt. 22:34-40.
Light: Ps. 27-1, Ps. 119:105, Matt. 5:14, John 1:4.
Loneliness: Hebrews: 13:5-19.
Love: Deut. 6:5, Ps. 73:25-26, Lev. 19:18, 1 Cor. 13:4-8, 13.
Money: Jer. 17:11, Job 31:24-25, Luke 16:8-15, Matt. 19:21-26.
Motherhood: Ex. 20:12, Prov. 1:8, Prov. 10:1, Prov. 15:20, Prov. 23:22, Prov. 29:15.
Obeying: Ex. 19:5, John 10:27, John 14:15, Acts 5:29, John 5:3.
Old age: Gen. 47:9, Deut. 34:7, 2 Sam. 19:34-37.
Parents: Hebrews 12:5-13, Luke 2:41-50.
Patience: Hebrews 10:36.
Patriotism: Matt. 5:1-10, Jer. 1:6, Jer. 20:2, Jer. 37:15-16.
Peace: Ps. 133:1, Prov. 11:17, Prov. 20:3, Matt. 5:9, 1 Cor. 14:33, Col. 1:2.
Pentecost: Acts 2:2-4, Acts 4:8, John 14:16.
Poverty: Prov. 15:16, Prov. 24:33-34.
Prayer: Luke 11:2-4, Matt. 6:5-15.
Pride: 1 Kings 20:11, Prov. 25:14, 1 Cor. 8:1.
Recreation: Mark 6:31, Mark 7:24.
Responsibility: Luke 21:1-4, John 15:22-24, Matt. 12:41.
Rest: Gen. 2:2-3, Deut. 28:63-68, Heb. 3:7.
Revenge: Matt. 5:38-42, Luke 6:29-30.
Salvation: Ex. 15:2, John 3:14-17, John 5:24.
Self-awareness: Ex. 13:15, John 1:19-23.
Teachers: Solomon 6:12-20, Luke 20:20-26.
Thanksgiving: Matt. 15:32-39, Ps. 50:14, Ps. 106:1, 1 Thess. 5:18.
Time: Ps. 90:9-10, Rom. 13:11-12, John 16:16.
Trouble: Romans 8:28, Romans 31, John 14:1.
Truth: Ps. 51:6, Ps. 89:14, Ps. 100:5, Prov. 12-19, John 14:6, John 16:13.
War: Ex. 17:1-16, Jos. 1:1-10, 1 Kings 7:9-12, 1 Thess. 4:16, Matt. 24:4-14, Eph. 6:10-17.
Witness: Is. 49:6, John 1:1-8.

MUSIC BIBLIOGRAPHY

Psalms:

Deiss, Lucien. *Biblical Hymns and Psalms.* World Library of Sacred Music, Inc., Cincinnati, Ohio, 1965.

Gelineau, Joseph. *Twenty-four Psalms and a Canticle.* Gregorian Institute of America, Toledo, Ohio, 1965.

Folk Hymns (Printed and recorded music is available for most selections cited below):

American Folk Song Mass. Father Ian Mitchell, FEL Publications, Ltd., Chicago, Ill.

Alley. Ray Repp. FEL Publications, Ltd., Chicago, Ill., 1968, Cat. No. 032.

Come Alive With Ray Repp. Ray Repp, FEL Publications, Ltd., Chicago, Ill., 1969, Cat. No. 072.

Come Out! Neil Blunt and Jack Miffleton, World Library of Sacred Music, Inc., Cincinnati, Ohio, 1971, Cat. No. FR-2382-SM.

Concert of Sacred Music. Duke Ellington, RCA Records, New York, Cat. No. 3582.

Discover and Create. Paul and Barbara Abels, Friendship Press, New York, 1968.

Father Rivers Sings the Music. "Music for Christian Unity," by Jan Vermulst.

F.E.L. Hymnal. FEL Church Publications, Ltd., Chicago, Ill., 1968.

For Heaven's Sake. Helen Kromer and Frederick Silver, Kingsway Records, Williamson Music, Inc., New York, 1961.

Freeing the Spirit. National Office for Black Catholics, 734 15 St., NW, Washington, D.C.

Gonna Sing My Lord. Joe Wise, World Library of Sacred Music, Inc., Cincinnati, Ohio, 1967, Cat. No. ESA-1348-1.

Hand In Hand. Joe Wise, World Library of Sacred Music, Inc., Cincinnati, Ohio, 1968, Cat. No. ESA-1741-1.

Hi God! Rev. Carey Landry and Carol Jean Kinghorn, North American Liturgy Resources, Cincinnati, Ohio, 1973.

Hymnal for Young Christians. Ray Repp, Father Rivers, Sister Germaine, Medical Mission Sisters, et al., FEL Church Publications, Chicago, Ohio.

Hymns for Now. Workers Quarterly, 875 North Dearborn St., Chicago, Ill., July, 1967.

I've Been in the Storm for So Long. Father Rivers, World Library of Sacred Music, Ohio.

Joy is Like the Rain. Sister Miriam Theresa Winter, Vanguard Music Corporation, New York and Avant Garde Records, New York, Cat. No. AVM-10M.

Let's Sing Together. Geneva Press, Philadelphia, 1965.

Let Us Pray. Volumes 1 to 6. Robert Heyer, Jean Marie Hiesberger, Bernadette Kenny, Paulist Press, New York, N.Y. and Paramus, N.J., 1972.

Like Olive Branches, Lucien Diess, World Library of Sacred Music, Cincinnati, Ohio.

Mass For Young Americans. Ray Repp, FEL Church Publications, Inc., Chicago, Ohio, Cat. No. 810F-6403.

Missa Ala Samba. Alexander Pelequin, World Music Library, Cincinnati, Ohio.

Missa Bossa Nova. Peter Scholtes, FEL Publications, Inc., Chicago, Ill.

Nine Carols for Ballads, Sydney Carter, Clarion Phonographic Services, Ltd., London, 1964.

Run, Come, See! Robert Blue, FEL Publications, Ltd., Chicago, Illinois, 1966.

Run Like a Deer. Paul Quinlan, FEL Publications, Chicago, Ill.

Sing Praise! Sing Praise to God. Ray Repp, FEL Publications, Inc., Chicago, Ill.

Songs of Protest and Love. Ian Mitchell, FEL Publications, Chicago, Ill.

Songs In Celebration. Lucien Deiss, World Library of Sacred Music., Cincinnati, Ohio.

Songs of Many Nations. Cooperative Recreation Service, Delaware, Ohio, 1962.

Songs of the New Creation. Dameans, FEL Publications, Ltd., Chicago, Ill., 1970.

Songs of Salvation. Sister Germaine, FEL Publications, Ltd., Chicago, Ill., 1966.

Songs for Young Children. Mary Lu Walker, Paulist Press, New York, N.Y./Paramus, N.J.

Songs for Today. Ewald Bash and John Yluisaker, Youth Department, American Lutheran Church, Minneapolis, Minn., 1965.

They'll Know We Are Christians. Peter Scholtes, FEL Publications, Inc., Chicago, Ill.

Tell the World. Dameans, FEL Publications, Ltd., Chicago, Ill., 1969.
Ten New Songs. Sydney Carter, Clarion Phonographic Services, Ltd., London, Eng.
Twentieth Century Folk Mass. Father Geoffrey Beaumont, Joseph Weinberger, Ltd., London, 1958.
Twenty-One Hymn Tunes, Joseph Weinberger, Ltd., London, 1966.
Watch With Me. Joe Wise, Fontaine House, North American Liturgy Resources, Cincinnati, Ohio, 1973.
The Winds of God. Frederick H. Gore and Milton H. Wilhams, Vanguard Music Corporation, New York.
With Steel and Strings. Jack Miffleton, World Library of Sacred Music, Inc., Cincinnati, Ohio.
With Joyful Lips. Lucien Diess, World Library of Sacred Music, Cincinnati, Ohio.
Women of the Old Testament. Sarah Hershberg, FEL Publications, Chicago, Ill.
Young People's Hymnal. Joe Wise, Sebastian Temple, Lucien Diess, Jack Miffleton, Tom Parket, et al., World Library of Sacred Music, Inc., Cincinnati, Ohio, 1969.

Contemporary Folk Rock Songs:

"All Things Must Pass," George Harrison, Harrison's Music, Inc., New York, 1972.
"Bridge Over Troubled Water," Simon and Garfunkel, Charing Cross Music, New York and Columbia Records, N.Y., 1970.
"Chelsea Morning," Joni Mitchell, Siquomb Publishing Corp., New York, 1970.
"Daniel," Elton John, M.C.B., Inc., 1973.
"Don Quixote," Gordon Lightfoot, Moose Music, Burbank, Cal., 1972.
"Don Quixote." Gordon Lightfoot, Warner Brothers Records, Inc., Burbank, Cal., 1972.
Fiddler on the Roof (sound track). Valando Music Inc., New York.
"I Am a Rock," Simon and Garfunkel, Electric Music Co., N.Y., 1965.
"I'll Catch the Sun," Rod McKuen, Cheval-Stanyan, Co., Hollywood, Cal., 1968.
"Morning Has Broken," Cat Stevens, North American Publishers Corp., Hialeah, Fla., 1972.
"My Sweet Lord," George Harrison, Harrison's Music, Inc., 1972.
"Sabbath Prayer," from *Fiddler On the Roof*, Valando Music, Inc., New York.
"Sit Down Young Stranger," Gordon Lightfoot, Moose Music, New York, 1968.

"Sometimes," Henry Mancini, North American Publishers Corp., Hialeah, Fla.

Sounds of Silence. Simon and Garfunkel, Columbia Records, Inc., New York, 1965.

Teaser and the Firecat. Cat Stevens, Island Records, Ltd., London & A&M Records, Cal.

"You Are the Sunshine of My Life," Stevie Wonder, Tamla, Inc., New York, 1973.

"You've Got A Friend," Carole King, Charles Hansen Music Books, New York, 1973.

Classical Music:

Mozart, Piano Concerto, K 467, C Major, Second Movement
Chopin, Concerto No. 1, Second Movement
Brahms, First Symphony, Second Movement
Sibelius, Swans of Tuonela, any selection
Mozart, Concerto, K491 in C Minor, Second Movement
Pachelbel, Canon in D Major MHS
Handel, *Messiah*, "Behold the Lamb of God."

BIBLIOGRAPHY

Periodicals

Liturgy Newsletters:
"Liturgy," publication of Liturgical Conference, Washington, D.C.
"Liturgy," publication of National Office of Black Catholics, 734 15th St., N.W., Washington, D.C. 20005.
"Celebration," publication of Children's Liturgy Committee, Box 2108, Baton Rouge, Louisiana 70821.

Catechetical Journals:
Religion Teachers' Journal, XXIII Publications, West Mystic, Conn.
The Catechist, George A. Pflaum Co., 38 West 5th St., Dayton, Ohio.
The Living Light, O.S.V. Publishers, Huntington, Indiana 46750.

Selected Articles

The Catechist (George Pflaum Co.)
Vol. 1, #6, March, 1968. Entire issue on celebration.
Vol. 2, #4, January, 1969. Teen Celebration on Brotherhood.
Vol. 3, #2, October, 1969. Primary grades: Prayers children pray.
Vol. 5, #6, March, 1972, Primary and intermediate children's mass for Pentecost and creative liturgical experiences for teens.

Religion Teachers' Journal (XXIII Publications)
Vol. 2, #10, January, 1969. "Make Your Own Liturgies."
Vol. 4, #1, February, 1970. "A Christmas Seder."
Vol 4, #4, May, 1970. "A Catechetical Liturgy Room."
Vol. 4, #7, October, 1970. "Praise the Lord With Banners."
Vol. 4, #9, January, 1971. "A Celebration for Small Children." "Preparing for the Bread of Life."
Vol. 5, #9, January, 1972. "A Living Liturgical Experience for 5th Graders."

Audio-Visual Material

Basic Resources:
Teleketics, Franciscan Communication Center, Los Angeles, Cal.
Paulist/Newman Press, 400 Sette Drive, Paramus, N.J. 07652.

Slideas, Loyola University Press, Chicago, Illinois.
Alba House Communications, Canfield, Ohio 44406.
Argus Publishers, 3505 North Ashland, Chicago, Ill. 60657.

Specific Resources:
"A Time To Die" (16mm film on death/resurrection), New Life Films, Kansas City, Mo.
"Christ Nourishes the Members of God's Family" (First Communion filmstrip), Benziger Co., New York.
"Everything Is Prayer" (poster, multimedia), Pflaum Co., 38 W. 5th St., Dayton, Ohio.

Sacramental Materials

"Christ Nourishes the Members of God's Family." New York: Benziger Co.
"I Prepare for Holy Communion." Collegeville, Minn.: Liturgical Press.
"It's All About Celebrating." Minneapolis, Minn.: Mine Publications.
"Meaning of the Sacraments." Dayton, Ohio: Pflaum/Standard.
"We Celebrate the Eucharist." Morristown, New Jersey: Silver Burdett.

Resource Manuals

Avery. *The Experimental Liturgy Book*. New York: Herder and Herder.
Benson. *Electric Liturgy*. Richmond, Va.: John Knox Press.
Benson. *Let It Run*. Richmond, Va.: John Knox Press.
Brown, John. *New Ways in Worship for Youth*. Valley Forge: Judson Press.
Deiss and Weyman. *Dancing for God*. Cincinnati, Ohio: World Library of Sacred Music.
Gallen. *Eucharistic Liturgies*. Paramus, N.J.: Paulist Press.
Moser. *Home Liturgies*. Paramus, N.J.: Paulist Press.
Weishert. *61 Gospel Talks for Children*. St. Louis: Concordia Publications.
Children's Liturgies. Washington, D.C.: The Liturgical Conference.

Background Reading

Horn, Henry E. *Worship In Crisis*. Philadelphia: Fortress Press.
Rochelle, J. C. *Create and Celebrate*. Philadelphia: Fortress Press.
Synder, Ross. *Contemporary Celebration*. Nashville: Abingdon Press.
Wilkins, R. J. *Understanding Christian Worship*. Dubuque, Iowa: Wm. C. Brown, Co.

Readings and Prayers

Pre-school and elementary children:
Arch Books. St. Louis, Mo.: Concordia Press.
Children's Bible. St. Meinrad, Ind.: Liturgical Press.
Golden Children's Bible. New York: Western Publishing Co.
Frederic. Leo Lionni. New York: Pantheon (Random House). Also in movie version.
Rejoice Books. Paramus, N.J.: Paulist/Newman Press.
Swimmy. Leo Lionni. New York: Pantheon (Random House).
The Giving Tree. Shel Silverstein. New York: Harper and Row.
99 Plus One. Pottebaum. Minneapolis: Augsburg Press.

Junior and senior high students:
The Giving Tree. Shel Silverstein. New York: Harper and Row.
He Is The Still Point/Take Off Your Shoes and others. Chicago: Argus Press.
Jonathan Livingston Seagull. R. Bach. New York: Macmillan.
The Little Prince. Antoine de St. Exupéry. New York: Harcourt, Brace and World.
Listen to Love and *Faces of Freedom.* Winona, Minn.: St. Mary's Press.
The Prophet. Kahlil Gibran, New York: Alfred A. Knopf, Publishers.
The Velveteen Rabbit. Margery Williams. New York: Doubleday.